T0294638

AUTHENTICITY

AUTHENTICITY

Understanding Misinformation Through the Study of Heritage Tourism

William Aspray and James W. Cortada

ROWMAN & LITTLEFIELD
LANHAM · BOULDER · NEW YORK · LONDON

Published by Rowman & Littlefield
An imprint of The Rowman & Littlefield Publishing Group, Inc.
4501 Forbes Boulevard, Suite 200, Lanham, Maryland 20706
www.rowman.com

86-90 Paul Street, London, EC2A 4NE

British Library Cataloguing in Publication Information Available

Library of Congress Cataloging-in-Publication Data Available

ISBN 978-1-53817-235-3 (cloth)
ISBN 978-1-53817-264-3 (paperback)
ISBN 978-1-53817-236-0 (e-book)

♾™ The paper used in this publication meets the minimum requirements of American National Standard for Information Sciences—Permanence of Paper for Printed Library Materials, ANSI/NISO Z39.48-1992.

CONTENTS

PREFACE

Since the 2016 US presidential election, there has been an outpouring of scholarship on misinformation. We two authors, together and separately, have been adding to that literature, drawing upon our strengths in history and information studies, to fill gaps in the literature, for example, showing how misinformation is not a recent phenomenon but instead has been common in American public life since the nation's founding; explaining how political fact-checking has a complex history that emerged at about the same time as the Internet; and examining how certain institutions, such as libraries and museums, have been involved in debunking false claims and educating the public.[1] The reliability of information has become an important issue in modern society, and it is increasingly becoming evident that authenticity of sources, facts, and points of view plays a significant role. So, the discussion about misinformation increasingly needs to be viewed through the lens of authenticity—a topic that has not been studied as thoroughly as other aspects of truth. This book examines authenticity by examining three cases studies of heritage tourism, and then connects the topic to the wider issue of misinformation.

What do we mean by these terms? We will discuss in considerable detail in chapter 1 what *authenticity* means. For now, let us consider the definitions in the *Merriam-Webster Dictionary*. It defines "authenticity" as: "worthy of acceptance or belief as conforming to or based on fact," "conforming to an original so as to reproduce essential features," "made or done the same way as an original," "true to one's own personality, spirit, or character," and "not false or imitation."[2] Thus authenticity can be about both an original artifact and a reproduction. *Merriam-Webster* defines *mis-information*[3] as "incorrect or misleading information," where *information* is defined as "knowledge obtained from investigation, study, or instruction" or simply "facts, data."[4] Information scientists make distinctions between wisdom, knowledge, information, and data in their widely disseminated pyramid of information,[5] but these distinctions are not important to our discussion in this book. *Merriam-Webster* does not define *heritage tourism* but it does define *heritage* as "something transmitted by or acquired from a predecessor" or "something possessed as a result of one's natural situation or birth" and as a word that has close connections with other words including *legacy, inheritance, tradition,* and *birthright.*[6] We believe the main definition in *Merriam-Webster* for *tourism* ("the practice of traveling for recreation")[7] does not apply well here because heritage tourism is as much or more about traveling for educational purposes as for recreational purposes. The tourism industry defines heritage tourism in a way that works better for us: "The National Trust for Historic Preservation defines heritage tourism as 'traveling to experience the places, artifacts, and activities that authentically represent the stories and people of the past and present.'"[8]

Why choose heritage tourism as a means to study authenticity? One of the most rapidly growing academic professions in North America and Western Europe is leisure and tourism studies. Scholars in this field have been quite active over the past fifty years (but especially in the past decade) in understanding questions of authenticity and inauthenticity as it pertains to heritage tourism sites. They have arrived at several powerful conceptual approaches that can readily be applied by information scholars. Our aim in this book is to identify ways in which the conceptual approaches to heritage tourism studies can be applied by information scholars to gain new insights into the study of misinformation. We do this through two chapters focused on key concepts from heritage tourism studies, together with three chapters focused on case studies: of one small heritage site (Lindsborg, Kansas, often known as "Little Sweden, USA"), one large private heritage site (Colonial Williamsburg, Virginia), and one large public site (Gettysburg, Pennsylvania). Not only do these case studies focus on different aspects of authenticity and misinformation, all three have already been widely studied by other scholars (for other purposes), so we can draw upon their fieldwork to enrich our analysis. A final chapter pulls together what we have learned from the case studies and the examination of the heritage tourism literature and explains how this is relevant to enriching the study of misinformation.

There are, of course, thousands of other heritage tourism sites that are destinations for Americans, located across the United States and in other countries. Think, for example, of American citizens who visit Ireland or Africa to explore their family roots; or who visit the Normandy region in France to appreciate where family members participated in the Allied invasion during the Second World War. We are not attempting to be comprehensive in the tourism sites we study. Instead, we have focused on just three because we believe that a careful study of them reveals many of the key issues that are related to the authenticity of artifacts, narratives, and environments and how they are connected to a wide variety of other issues such as local economy, civil strife, ethnic heritage, American patriotism, and personal identity.

We believe that misinformation is increasingly common and relevant in political discourse, especially with the rise of autocracy and the threat to democracy. While there is a growing literature on heritage tourism studies, researchers are just beginning to study the connection between inauthenticity and misinformation—and to try to show how to better study the latter using methods developed to study the former. This book will appeal to scholars who are interested in heritage tourism, which includes not only tourism scholars but also some anthropologists, sociologists, geographers, and management information scholars. This book should provide useful perspective to those who are following the current messy row about how to tell the story of President James Madison's home, Montpelier, debated by those who want to emphasize it as where the U.S. Constitution was written or where hundreds of slaves worked. These kinds of debates arise regularly as we Americans try to come to terms with our complex past. It will also be of interest to information scholars and others such as computer scientists and linguists who have been studying misinformation. The parts of this book that address the disruptive effect of the Internet will be of interest to media and communication scholars. This book was written avoiding academic jargon, and it connects with issues of relevance to all Americans about their heritage—in fact, many readers will have visited the heritage sites we study; so, this book is appropriate for public libraries and is readily accessible to an educated general reader. Finally, this book may be assigned in an undergraduate or graduate hospitality course in a school that prepares people for careers in tourism.

We, the authors, are senior fellows at the Charles Babbage Institute, a research institute for the study of computing, information, and culture at the University of Minnesota Twin Cities. We both received PhDs in history and both have been studying information and its history for many years. We are both seasoned authors, each having written or edited dozens of books. Aspray has a previous life as a professor and nonprofit center director, while Cortada had a long career in sales, consulting, research, management, and executive positions at the IBM Corporation.

The publishing team at Rowman & Littlefield has, once again, supported our work, doing their usual excellent work. Our editor, Charles Harmon, helped us shape this book and then, with his colleagues Erinn Slanina, Jaylene Perez, and Amelia Manasterli shepherded it to publication.

NOTES

1. James W. Cortada and William Aspray, *Fake News Nation: The Long History of Lies and Misrepresentations in America* (Lanham, MD: Rowman & Littlefield, 2019); William Aspray and James W. Cortada, *From Urban Legends to Political Fact-Checking: Online Scrutiny in America, 1990–2015* (New York: Springer, 2019); William Aspray, *Making and Debunking Myths About the Old West: A Case Study of Misinformation for Information Scholars, Information & Culture* 56, no. 3 (2021): 251–78; James W. Cortada and William Aspray, "Gaining Historical Perspective on Political Fact-Checking (with James Cortada)," *Library and Information Science Research (LIBRES)* 30, no. 1 (2020): 1–33; and James W. Cortada and William Aspray, "The Magic of Debunking: Interrogating Fake Facts in the United States Since the Eighteenth Century," *Library and Information History* 35, no. 3 (2019): 133–50.

2. *Merriam-Webster Online*, s.v. "authentic," https://www.merriam-webster .com/dictionary/authentic (accessed March 29, 2022).

3. *Merriam-Webster Online*, s.v. "misinformation," https://www.merriam -webster.com/dictionary/misinformation (accessed March 29, 2022). Chapter 1 in Cortada and Aspray, *Fake News Nation* provides definitions to many terms conceptually related to misinformation.

4. *Merriam-Webster Online*, s.v. "information," https://www.merriam-web-ster.com/dictionary/information (accessed March 29, 2022).

5. See, for example, Charles H. Davis and Debora Shaw, eds., *Introduction to Information Science and Technology* (Medford, NJ: Information Today, 2011), 12–13.

6. *Merriam-Webster Online*, s.v. "heritage," https://www.merriam-webster .com/dictionary/heritage (accessed March 29, 2022).

7. *Merriam-Webster Online*, s.v. "tourism," https://www.merriam-webster .com/dictionary/tourism (accessed March 29, 2022).

8. Advisory Council on Historic Preservation, Heritage Tourism, https:// www.achp.gov/heritage_tourism (accessed March 29, 2022).

1

AUTHENTICITY AND MISINFORMATION IN THE AMERICAN HISTORICAL EXPERIENCE

We're hamstrung by these historical societies and tourist boards. They're all a load of bloody romantics as far as I can see, It's all a myth. The past wasn't like that; it wasn't neat and tidy like they all seem to think.[1]

The issue of authenticity runs, like an obligato, through tourism studies.[2]

In the late 1980s, Peter Shaffer's comedic play, *Lettice and Lovage*, was the talk of London's West End. Dame Maggie Smith, for whom the play was written, did not play a schoolteacher in her prime[3] or a dowager countess[4] but, instead, a frustrated tour guide, Lettice Douffet, working in Fustian House in countryside England. To relieve her frustration, during her tours she increasingly embellished the history of the estate, a place where seemingly nothing had happened throughout the home's five-hundred-year history. Lettice's nemesis, Lotte Schoen, played by Margaret Tyzack, was an officer of the Preservation Trust who insisted that all information presented by her tour guides be factually correct. This play was essentially about a battle between truth and misinformation (introduced for entertainment's sake), in particular about portraying a heritage tourist site inauthentically. (We will return to Lettice in later chapters.)

In the conclusion to our book, *From Urban Legends to Political Fact-Checking*,[5] we suggested that the relationship between authenticity and misinformation merits further discussion. Authenticity is a kind of truth to self,[6] and the consumers of culture scrutinize cultural artifacts to determine whether they are authentic and sometimes become dissatisfied if they find the authenticity wanting. Since 1936, when the literary critic Walter Benjamin published his famous essay, "The Work of Art in the Age of Mechanical Reproduction,"[7] art and literature scholars, philosophers, and some historians—but few information scholars—have explored issues about the differences between original artworks and copies, between artistic creation and forgery.[8] There has similarly been study of the reception by the consumers of the artwork, for example, the reader of the book or the audience member at a play performance, who might question how authentically the author has rendered the setting or the personalities of the individual characters, and how this affects the audience's satisfaction with the work of art.

The scholarship about fakery in art and literature is moderately well known—even if it deserves further attention by information scholars—so, in this book we focus instead on a similar but distinct experience, which in the past quarter century has begun to be studied by the emerging academic discipline of tourism studies.[9] People who take tours of historic houses are participants in what James Cortada has called the *informed vacation*, during which the vacationer wants to be educated, not merely to relax.[10] There are many examples of informed vacations. Going on foreign tour and the Chautauqua seminars are two well-known examples from the nineteenth century. In the United States, another example that is of particular interest here is *heritage tourism*—of visiting, as tourists, towns that have a strong historical affiliation with a particular national or ethnic identity or sites in which something historically important happened. A similar kind of scrutiny of authenticity comes into play when one visits these sites, interacts with their guides, and buys the period furniture, tools, clothing, or musical instruments that are sold in their gift shops.

Tourism and leisure studies is one of the fastest growing academic disciplines of the past quarter century. In part, it is based in business and management ways of thinking.[11] But it is also based in cultural anthropology and other social sciences, and it is from this latter aspect that we will draw mainly in this book.[12] Tourism and leisure studies is a discipline that has received limited attention from information scholars, and yet there are considerable information phenomena involved in leisure and tourist activities. By examining the scholarship in tourism studies, the information scholar gains access to new case studies as well as to new frameworks, concepts, and theories that one can apply in order to enrich information studies. In particular, we focus in this book on the issue of (in)authenticity and its connection to misinformation.[13] While our primary audience is information scholars, we have written in a way to make this study more accessible to the interested tourism scholar or to the educated general reader.

The type of myth that is prevalent in these heritage tourism towns is historical myth, as opposed to etiological (causation/origination) myth or psychological myth.[14] The purpose of historical myths is to keep memory of a particular way of life alive. An historical myth might distort the facts, but some might regard this as acceptable if the myth helps to keep the memory intact. Anthropologists or folklore scholars are more interested in the meaning and the ways in which meaning is created and sustained; while the information scholar is more interested in learning in this setting about the information and misinformation that is created, by whom, in what ways, for what reasons, and which reactions people may have to this misinformation.

In this chapter, we provide an account of how ordinary people think about the authenticity of artifacts and places that are connected with American history. We then provide some examples of theorizing by scholars interested in heritage tourism. Chapter 2 reviews the scholarly tourism literature more systematically to identify the various ways in which scholars have thought about authenticity and how this thinking has changed over time. This chapter shares the results of a literature review of how information scholars study misinformation; and draws some conclusions about what information scholars can learn about misinformation from the tourism literature about authenticity and from the ethnographies of these cultural heritage towns, as well as potential next steps for academic study. In the next three chapters, we provide case studies of heritage tourism sites and how to think about their authenticity. We have selected three common types of cultural heritage sites for study in our three case studies. Chapter 3 identifies some of the small, private heritage tourism sites, in particular the small American towns that trade upon their ethnic cultural heritage to attract tourists and the ways in which they do so. After a general discussion, we focus on Lindsborg, Kansas, a town known widely as "Little Sweden, USA." Chapter 4 considers a larger private heritage site (Colonial Williamsburg in Virginia), and chapter 5 provides a case study of a large heritage site (Gettysburg in Pennsylvania) managed by a public entity, the National Park Service. The final chapter pulls this material together and presents findings for various audiences: information scholars, tourism scholars, and other academic disciplines interested in heritage tourism, tourism managers, and the general public. This book is a continuation of our series of studies on misinformation as seen from the lens of the information studies scholar.[15]

Let us begin this discussion by contrasting the three types of heritage tourism sites that we study. Some overall information about these types of heritage sites is given in table 1.1.

AUTHENTICITY IN THE AMERICAN HISTORICAL EXPERIENCE

When people scrutinize, one concern is for authenticity, whether the information or experience seems "authentic" or "real." But what is authenticity? Is it merely the inherent state of something being real or true, of being worthy of acceptance or belief? Is it the opposite of being false, fake, an imitation? Is it about being true to one's values or personality? Is Willie Nelson's music authentically American country and western? Is a fifth-generation Wisconsin farmer an authentic Midwestern farmer? Because one of your authors was baptized and confirmed in the Catholic Church does that make him an authentic Catholic, inasmuch as his parish priest wonders why he is an irregular attendant at Sunday mass? Many sociologists, anthropologists, historians, and others believe that authenticity is socially constructed, which is to say, not something intrinsic but instead identified by individuals and groups as being authentic. For these scholars, there is no absolute benchmark or scientific standard by which to determine authenticity; and the process of authenticating is at least as important as the final judgment as to whether something is authentic.

Throughout their history, Americans have identified with ethnic and geographically situated groups. A German immigrant in nineteenth-century Minnesota would accept a German immigrant living in Wisconsin as an authentic German or Midwesterner, because of their

Table 1.1 Types of Heritage Sites

Features	Coalition Model	Corporatist Model	National Model
Description	Community nonprofits agree to collaborate (e.g., Chambers of Commerce, civic organizations, local historical societies, interested individuals)	Single organization owns and manages (e.g., a foundation or a company)	Government-owned and -run, based on national politics, policies, and historical significance
Purpose	Local economic development, sustain pride of place, ethnic or regional identity	Promote patriotism or theme, not necessarily profitable but desirable that it be economically self-sustaining	Promote patriotism, educate the nation on history
Funding	Local government, grants from local civic groups, donations, admission fees to events	Major donations from corporations and wealthy individuals, broad public fundraising, admission fees, profits from gift shops	Federal government salaries and budgets, broad public fundraising, admission fees, profits from gift shops
Examples	"Little Sweden," Lindsborg, Kansas; Fredericksburg, Texas; New Glarus, Wisconsin	Colonial Williamsburg, Henry Ford Museum of American Innovation	Gettysburg Military Park, White House
Information and Messaging Style	Market promotion, advertising, festivals; loosely accurate; fragmented messaging; limited academic influence	Marketing, tours, museum exhibits, research-based publications, lectures; focused, disciplined; extensive academic influence	Tours, museum exhibits, lectures, research-based publications, rigorously accurate but conforming to national expectations; professionally trained scholars
Influencers	Various local community groups and businesses	Beholden to owner's messaging priorities, much like a corporate business model	Congress, cabinet-level department managerial practices, political inclinations; public, less so scholars

shared values, language, practices, and worldviews. These immigrant groups did not generally live in a closed society; instead, they allowed practices and identities of others to weave into their own, providing an elastic practice in how one identified with a group or set of activities.[16] Objects are sometimes considered authentic if they are made or used by groups that are regarded as being linked to these objects, such as Pueblo Indian pots; blues music if played by African American musicians raised in the Mississippi Delta, New Orleans, or Chicago; or country and western music if it originated in the South or parts of the West; or if they reflect styles associated with those places. This was typical American behavior throughout the nineteenth and twentieth centuries.[17]

People, too, created images of themselves as being authentic members of some particular group.[18] Thomas Jefferson created an image for himself as an advocate for rural life governed by minimal government administration, even though he was actually a college graduate who had lived in Europe and who was a familiar figure among the political and economic elite of his day. President Andrew Jackson created an image of himself in the 1820s as an Indian fighter and rough-and-tumble Westerner—despite the fact that he and his wife Rachel decorated their home in Nashville in a style that would have been approved by the salon divas of London or Paris. Many other examples can be found throughout American history. More recently, singer Loretta Lynn created an image of being an Appalachian miner's daughter. In time, Jefferson, the Jacksons, and Lynn were all regarded as authentic examples of the persona they presented. They promoted points of view that fit the public image of what people should look and act like as a rural president in the early 1800s, an up-and-coming Western politician in the 1820s, or a poor country singer in the mid-twentieth century who became wealthy in the process.[19]

Individual objects and events are associated with the notion of authenticity. A pot made by a Pueblo Indian sold to a tourist is said to be authentic, but not so if on its bottom is stamped "Made in China." Music is thought to be authentic if played by people who dress, act like, and come from that part of the country that people think of as the source of this kind of music. A New Yorker who excels at playing Appalachian banjo music faces a cognitive dissonance challenge in being accepted as authentic, whereas a less gifted player who grew up in the Blue Ridge Mountains is more likely to be accepted as authentic.

Decisions about what is real or not, what is authentic, have been made throughout American history—it is a form of personal scrutiny. Not until the rise of professional experts and scholars—largely beginning after the Civil War and expanding massively after the Second World War—did Americans begin to pass on to others the task of determining what is authentic and hence trustworthy.[20] Long before fact-checkers were working on the Internet, Americans carried out their own scrutiny or turned to others to carry out that task for them. Richard A. Peterson, a leading expert on authenticity, has linked the concept to fact-checking: "end users have more of a voice in authentication initially, but that the most visible keepers of collective memory, the critics, historians, archivists, teachers, documentary makers, music reissue specialists and the like, are increasingly important in enunciating the evolving idea of authenticity in any creative field as time goes by."[21] Folklorist Gary A. Fine speaks of these same people creating collective memories and even "reimaginations" of the past.[22]

American history is rife with reimagination. Today, one can see this process at work when visiting Jamestown or Williamsburg, Virginia, colonial villages from the 1600s and mid-1700s, respectively, but reconstructed only in the twentieth century. With the development of photography in the mid-nineteenth century, new forms of reimagination became possible, and with them new ways of being misled, resulting in the need for new kinds of experts to evaluate and sometimes expose them. During the Civil War, for example, photographers took pictures of battlefields. On occasion, to create more dramatic scenes, they would rearrange the placement of the dead bodies. For example, the photographer Alexander Gardner relocated a dead sniper on a hill at the Gettysburg battlefield and mislabeled the dead Union soldier as Confederate.[23] Like fake videos that circulate on the Internet today, people believed that the images they saw in the 1800s were real. There was little questioning of these photos as having been forged. People believed they were unbiased and true—images as they really were. Nevertheless, historians later discredited the authenticity of some of Gardner's photographs.[24] Turn-of-the-twentieth-century photographs of urban teenage gangs were similarly staged, and later exposed by photographic experts. But these photos nevertheless seemed real at the time to the public, which increasingly lived in urban communities and heard stories from neighbors or the local press about victims of gang muggings.[25] What they heard from friends, neighbors, and the press shaped their views of what was real and true.

Apologists excused this behavior, for example calling these photographs "expressive, rather than as a strictly literal medium."[26] For over a century that is how American Indians were often presented in visual images to the public. Not until after the Second World War did debunkers begin the process of pointing out what *really* happened.[27] But, a backfire effect was often in play; despite, or even sometimes because of, the debunking of this visual evidence, Indians continued to be viewed as wild and savage—as those people who fought the cowboy and farmer; this portrayal became the legendary subject of many hundreds of Western movies and television episodes. Film and television made it easier for Americans to dig in their heels on what they believed was real and authentic about Indians, and public opinion did not shift until the last quarter of the twentieth century—some 150 years after photographers began taking still shots of Indians.[28]

Recognizing the role of authenticity in the handling of information represents a recently opened frontier in academic study; previous scholars have instead mostly focused more narrowly on its role as a manifestation of imitation.[29] In the Victorian era, for example, it became fashionable in upper-class homes to acquire furniture that replicated the styles of earlier periods, dating to the Renaissance or more recently to the US Federalist period of the early 1800s. A leading historian of imitation, Miles Orvell, has linked imitation and authenticity to literature, architecture, home furnishing, and advertisement from the late 1800s through the twentieth century. He uses the phrase "the real thing" as part of his discourse regarding authenticity, going beyond mere replication (*imitation* is his word) of such things as furniture and style of art. He has observed that when the opportunity has existed for fraud, what constituted authenticity became a consideration.[30] Experts were thus needed to authenticate a piece of furniture or the painter of a particular supposed masterpiece.

This same role is being played in the twenty-first century by fact-checkers. For historians and other kinds of fact-checkers, authenticity has focused primarily on physical objects. Historian Daniel Boorstin shifted the conversation to what he called "pseudo-events," which include the examination of journalism, advertising, public relations, movies, and tourism in the twentieth century.[31] Disneyworld, for instance, has included many less-than-authentic representations of American history. Late in the twentieth century, the Walt Disney Company wanted to create an American history park in northern

Virginia that would have been a monumental, idealized combination of historical representation and theme park. This is the kind of manifestation that Boorstin had in mind as he described the notion of idealized, something-less-than-realistic activity. By the 2010s, as social commentator Kurt Andersen has argued, most Americans live in an inauthentic world that he has called *Fantasyland*. Into that world were deposited fake news, lies in politics and advertising, and various public beliefs.[32] In this new setting, people determined with their imagination what constituted truth and reality. Andersen pointed to the acumen in TV humorist Stephen Colbert's remark:

> Who's *Britannica* to tell me the Panama Canal was finished in 1914? If I wanna say it happened in 1941, that's my right. I don't trust books— they're all fact, no heart.... Face it folks, we are a divided nation... divided between those who think with their head and those who *know* with their heart.... Because that's where the truth comes from, ladies and gentlemen—the gut.[33]

Andersen's response to Colbert's assessment was "*exactly*. America had changed in this particular, peculiar way."[34] One can think of fact-checkers in such an environment as being heroic figures shoveling sand against the incoming ocean tide, but unfortunately with what the writer Ernest Hemingway called their "crap detectors" as ineffective as children's shovels are at the beach.

In today's world, one could ask whether artificial intelligence (AI) is an imitation of the "real thing"—human brains doing the thinking. Do bots represent fake opinions? In the 1920s the American Management Association declared an end to a nearly century-long discussion about whether handmade or machine-made products were authentic, declaring that the best quality items were machine made. Is AI engendering the new "machine made" truths of our time? Already, there are reports that perhaps over half the items on the Internet are software creations.[35]

THEORIZING ABOUT AUTHENTICITY BY HERITAGE TOURISM SCHOLARS

In the previous section, we have discussed how the public thinks about authenticity in a commonsense way. This section presents some examples of the theorizing by heritage tourism scholars about authenticity.

We will learn more about this theorizing in chapter 2. We give the sense of what tourism scholars have to offer about authenticity by focusing here only on two papers by Athinodoros Chronis (one of them co-authored with Ronald Hampton),[36] and identify three basic ideas from these two papers.[37]

The first major idea is that authenticity is discussed by both tourists and the academic community in many different and sometimes confounding ways, but to gain a better perspective it helps to differentiate between two different aspects: authenticity as an experience and authenticity as a product feature. The former is subjective; it is about the emotional response that a tourist might have when they visit a heritage site as to whether they feel they have attained a good sense of what it is to live in the past by visiting the site. These subjective experiences may be different for different people, depending on their backgrounds and their reasons for choosing to visit this heritage site. So, the abiding question here is whether the tourist feels as though they know what it was like to live in this past they are interested in experiencing. The latter aspect is objective; it is a question of whether the site correctly portrays the heritage events through "real" artifacts, factually correct narratives, and historically faithful environments. So, the abiding question here is whether the artifacts, stories, and environment will pass muster when judged by experts such as historians or anthropologists against external criteria of historical accuracy.

The second major idea in these papers is that there are five different ways in which a heritage site manifests itself as authentic: *object-related authenticity* refers to the artifacts on the heritage site as those that actually appeared, for example on a battle site such as Gettysburg, and were the ones that were meaningful to the events that transpired there; *factual authenticity* refers to whether the events that are portrayed on the heritage site actually took place in the way they are presented; *personage authenticity* concerns whether real people from the historic time, for example, whether it was a famous figure such as Thomas Jefferson or an unidentified slave at Jefferson's estate Monticello, lived in this historical setting and acted in the way they are presented; *locational authenticity* refers to whether the re-enactment is in the exact location where the event actually occurred; and finally *contextual authenticity* concerns whether this environment has been rendered to give it "an unchanged, unmediated, and faithful environmental context,"[38] for example, a pastoral landscape not encroached upon by urbanization or industrialization at the edges of Colonial Williamsburg, or the absence of tourist gift shops detracting from a heritage site.

The third major idea in these papers concerns "tourism imaginaries" and how they are socially constructed. According to Chronis, "tourism imaginaries are defined as value-laden, emotion-conferring collective narrative constructions that are associated with and enacted in a particular place through tourism."[39] It is this "social construct that envelops and shapes an otherwise unassuming physical space into an evocative tourism destination."[40] The heritage tourist is not attracted to Gettysburg because it has the special scenery of, say, the Grand Canyon; instead, the tourist visits because of what happened there that interests them, whether that be military maneuvers, state rights, emancipation, or some other theme. Chronis identifies four elements that work together to create the imaginary. First, there is narrative. "We would probably have nothing meaningful to say about the past if not in the form of stories.... Each tale is comprised of a number of stories that say something about what happened in the past, who participated, and why. These narratives do not simply describe what happened in the past, but they make tourists' experiences meaningful."[41] Second, these stories are then provided with meaning by the effort to provide "moral valuation of the past."[42] Third is the reinforcement that comes through "emplaced enactment," in which the tourist engages in carrying out the imaginary. For example, as Chronis explains in the case of Gettysburg: "First, tourists at Gettysburg are located on the very ground where their ancestors had been standing and the experience of "being-there" adds material reality and ground to the imaginary. Second, as a sensory experience, Gettysburg can be touched, smelled, and walked on. Third, the embodied presence within the narrative space provides opportunities for embodied practices. Whether in the form of walking, following the steps of the combatants, or (re)enacting military formations, tourists are doing the imaginary."[43] Finally, the fourth step is emotional attachment between the story the heritage site tells and the tourist's everyday life. As Christos notes, "In numerous instances, tourists were deeply moved by the human agonizing that transpires through storytelling."[44]

Chronis makes two additional important points about the tourist imaginary. First, these historical imaginaries are "collective narrative constructions" that are not generally created separately by each individual tourist but instead are sites that generally become known as the place with some particular attribute or story line, for example,

Gettysburg "is clearly defined in the tourist domain as the town where the bloodiest battle of the Civil War took place."[45] Paradoxically, "Tourism imaginaries are seen as pliant certainties, that is, although they confer a powerful certainty as to what a tourism destination is, they are couched at the same time in pliant—even conflicting—narrative articulations.[46] Chronis amplifies on what he means by this:

> Since stories are not natural but human inventions, we cannot escape the challenge of multiple and even conflicting narratives. And we witness this in the tension between the tale of patriotic sacrifice and the tale of northern aggression. The presence of multiple tales is informative in that it deflects our focus from what the historical reality actually was and, instead, draws attention to the authors and readers of multiple, competing potentialities. Storytelling about Gettysburg is not merely the reporting of the events of the past as they happened and it does not capture the character of the place in any objective manner. As we know, narratives are characterized by selective appropriation of past events.[47]

NOTES

1. Peter Robinson, *A Dedicated Man* (New York: William Morrow, 1988).
2. G. Hughes, "Authenticity in Tourism," *Annals of Tourism Research* 22, no. 4 (1995): 781-803.
3. *The Prime of Miss Jean Brodie*, 1969, movie directed by Ronald Neame; based on a book by Muriel Spark of the same name (Philadelphia, PA: Lippincott, 1962).
4. *Downton Abbey*, television series, ITV, 2010-2016.
5. William Aspray and James W. Cortada, *From Urban Legends to Political Fact-Checking: Online Scrutiny in America, 1990-2015* (New York: Springer, 2019).
6. The language here is similar to a philosophical discussion that began in the eighteenth century and continues today, concerning what is an authentic truth to self for the human individual, given the pressures of society. The principal philosophers engaging this issue have been Martin Heidegger, in *Being and Time* (New York: Harper & Row, [1927] 1962), translated by J. Macquarrie and E. Robinson; and a vituperative criticism by Theodor Adorno, *The Jargon of Authenticity* (Northwestern University Press, [1964] 1973), translated by Knut Tarnowski and Frederic Will. For an excellent review of this philosophical literature see Varga, Somogy and Charles Guignon, "Authenticity," *The Stanford Encyclopedia of Philosophy* (2020, https://plato.stanford.edu/entries/authenticity/). Dave Harris notes that tourism scholars have followed an existentialist

line of argument when they speak of "existential authenticity" or "sincerity" but was dismissive of this scholarship, saying "I couldn't help thinking about the hoo-hah about authenticity in Tourism. Adorno would sort them out!" (Brief Notes on: Adorno, https://www.arasite.org/adjarg.html, accessed March 11, 2022). Examples of existentialist thought in tourism studies include: C. J. Steiner and Y. Reisinger, "Understanding Existential Authenticity," *Annals of Tourism Research* 33, no. 2 (April 2006): 299–318; Lorraine Brown, "Tourism: A Catalyst for Existential Authenticity," *Annals of Tourism* Research 40 (January 2013): 176–90; or Hyounggon Kim and Tazim Jamal, "Touristic Quest for Existential Authenticity," *Annals of Tourism Research* 34, no. 1 (January 2007): 181–201. It is beyond the scope of this book to trace the various connections between tourism studies and philosophy. We also wonder what Adorno would say about Andrew Potter's social criticism regarding authenticity in his book, *The Authenticity Hoax: Why the Real Things We See Don't Make Us Happy* (New York: HarperPerennial, 2011), which has a section with the same title as Adorno's book.

7. Walter Benjamin, *The Work of Art in the Age of Technological Reproducibility, and Other Writings on Media* (Cambridge, MA: Harvard University Press, 2008).

8. See, for example, Denis Dutton, *The Forger's Art: Forgery and the Philosophy of Art* (Berkeley: University of California Press, 1983); or Anthony Grafton, *Forgers and Critics: Creativity and Duplicity in Western Scholarship* (Princeton, NJ: Princeton University Press, 1990). For a look at these issues in the age of cryptocurrency and digital reproduction, see Annette Vee, "NFTs, Digital Scarcity, and the Computational Aura," *Interfaces: Essays and Reviews in Computing and Culture*, vol. 2 (Charles Babbage Institute, University of Minnesota, 2021), 38–54.

9. Taillon, *Understanding Tourism*.

10. James W. Cortada, *All the Facts: A History of Information in the United States Since 1870* (New York: Oxford, 2016), 212–18.

11. For example, Allison Morrison, Jack Carlsen, and Paul Weber, "Small Tourism Business Research Change and Evolution," *International Journal of Tourism Research* 12 (2010): 739–49 reviews and categorizes the business research concerning small tourism, which constitutes a major segment of the heritage tourism business. Craig Wiles, "Consideration of Historical Authenticity in Heritage Planning and Development," *Proceedings of the 2007 Northeastern Recreation Research Symposium*, GTR-NRS-P-23, https://www.nrs.fs.fed.us/pubs/gtr/gtr_nrs-p-23papers/41wiles-p23.pdf (accessed March 29, 2022) explores how beliefs about authenticity affect the products and services provided to visitors.

12. In a theoretical review of tourism studies scholarship, Tribe and Liburd argue that tourism studies has traditionally be seen as consisting of social

science (as examined by economics, geography, sociology, anthropology, psychology, political science, and law) and business ("vocational areas of operation, such as marketing, finance, human resource management, service management, destination planning, ITC and innovation") studies. They argue, however, in favor of a place in tourist studies for the humanities and the arts (philosophy, history, language, literature, communication, design, music, dance, and art) "that concern human expression and the study of culture." They also argue there is a role for the natural and applied science in tourist studies, but this was underdeveloped at the time of their paper (p. 48 in John Tribe and Janne J. Liburd, "The Tourist Knowledge System," *Annals of Tourism Research* 57 [2016]: 44–61).

13. The two authors of this paper, together with Andrew Dillon and Jenna Hartel, are currently working on a more general study on what information scholars can learn from tourism scholars, which goes beyond the issues of authenticity and misinformation.

14. For a brief, popular discussion of these different kinds of myths, see "The Three Types of Myths," *Mythology Unbound: An Online Textbook for Classical Mythology*, https://press.rebus.community/mythologyunbound/chapter/three-types-of-myth/ (accessed August 25, 2021). One definition of historical myth is given by Roland Bernhard et al. (*Historical Myth: A Definition from the Perspective of History Education*), https://www.academia.edu/39317435/Historical_myth_a_definition_from_the_perspective_of_history_education_research?from=cover_page (accessed December 21, 2021)): "The particular speciality of historical myths is the creation of narrative cohesion within a specific community and the reconnection of the present to a past that infuses it with meaning." There are many studies of historical myth and mythmaking, used across various areas of history, area studies, and anthropology. Some examples include: A. Nothnagle, "From Buchenwald to Bismarck: Historical Myth-Building in the German Democratic Republic, 1945–1989," *Central European History* (1993); K. Kaiser and J. M. Halpern, "Historical Myth and the Invention of Political Folklore in Contemporary Serbia," *Anthropology of East Europe Review* (1998); M. H. Williamson, "Pocahantas and Captain John Smith: Examining a Historical Myth," *History & Anthropology* (1992); and N. A. Skov, "The Use of Historical Myth, Denmark's World War II Experience Made to Serve Practical Goals," *Scandinavian Studies* (2000).

15. In addition to our book on urbans legends and political fact-checking, see James Cortada and William Aspray, *Fake News Nation* (Lanham, MD: Rowman & Littlefield, 2019); James Cortada and William Aspray, "The Magic of Debunking: Interrogating Fake Facts in the United States Since the Eighteenth Century," *Library and Information History* 35, no. 3 (2019): 133–50; William Aspray, "Making and Debunking Myths about the Old West: A Case Study of Misinformation for Information Scholars," *Information & Culture* 56 (2021):

251-78; and James W. Cortada and William Aspray, Gaining Historical Perspective on Political Fact-Checking (with James Cortada), *Library and Information Science Research (LIBRES)* 30, no. 1 (2020): 1-33.

16. Richard A. Peterson, "In Search of Authenticity," *Journal of Management Studies* 42, no. 5 (July 2005): 1086-87.

17. The study of who provided music and the origins of the music itself has, in particular, the subject of extensive study regarding authenticity in America. See, for example, M. A. Bufwack and R. K. Oermann, *Finding Her Voice: Women in Country Music, 1800-2000* (Nashville, TN: Vanderbilt University Press, 2003); R. D. Cohen, *Rainbow Quest: The Folk Music Revival and American Society, 1940-1970* (Amherst, MA: University of Massachusetts Press, 2002); D. Grazinian, *Blue Chicago: The Search for Authenticity in Urban Blues Clubs* (Chicago, IL: University of Chicago Press, 2003); R. A. Peterson, *Creating Country Music: Fabricating Authenticity* (Chicago, IL: University of Chicago Press, 1997).

18. E. Goffman, *The Presentation of Self in Everyday Life* (New York: Doubleday, 1959); D. E. Whistnant, *All that is Native and Fine: The Politics of Culture in an American Region* (Chapel Hill, NC: University of North Carolina Press, 1983).

19. For insight into the process, we have Loretta Lynn's own testimony in her memoirs, *Loretta Lynn: Coalminer's Daughter* (Chicago, IL: Regnery, 1976). More generally, this process of presenting oneself will be familiar to those who have read America's most widely read sociologist of the twentieth century, Erving Goffman, in his *The Presentation of Self in Everyday Life* (New York: Anchor, 1959).

20. For example, see Michael Kammen, *American Culture, American Tastes: Social Change and the 20th Century* (New York: Alfred A. Knopf, 1999), 3-46.

21. Peterson, "In Search of Authenticity," 1092.

22. Gary A. Fine, *Difficult Reputations: Collective Memories of the Evil, Inept, and Controversial* (Chicago, IL: University of Chicago Press, 2001), but see also his, *Everyday Genius: Self-Taught Art and the Culture of Authenticity* (Chicago, IL: University of Chicago Press, 2004).

23. Miles Orvell, *The Real Thing: Imitation and Authenticity in American Culture, 1880-1940* (Chapel Hill, NC: University of North Carolina Press, 1989), 95-97.

24. Orvell, *The Real Thing*.

25. Orvell, *The Real Thing*, 96-97.

26. Orvell, *The Real Thing*, 99.

27. See, for example, Joanna Cohan Sherer, "You Can't Believe Your Eyes: Inaccuracies in Photographs of North American Indians," *Studies in Visual Communication* 2, no. 2 (Fall 1975): 67-79; Zachary R. Jones, "Images of the Surreal: Contrived Photographs of Native American Indians in Archives and

Suggested Best Practices," *Journal of Western Archives* 6, no. 1 (2015): article 6, DOI: https://doi.org/10.26077/6ba8-92ae; Aleksandra Sherman, Lani Cupo, Nancy Marie Mithlo, "Perspective-Taking Increases Emotionality and Empathy but Does not Reduce Harmful Biases against American Indians: Converging Evidence from the Museum and Lab." *PLoS ONE* 15, no. 2 (2020): e0228784, https://doi.org/10.1371/journal.pone.0228784; D. W. Penney, L. A. Roberts, and N. Barr, *Images of Identity: American Indians in Photographs* (Detroit Institute of Art, 1994); and Steven Hoelscher, "Viewing Indians: Native Encounters with Power, Tourism, and the Camera in the Wisconsin Dells, 1866-1907," *American Indian Culture and Research Journal* 27, no. 4 (2003): 1–51.

28. For example, Christopher Lyman, *The Vanishing Race, and Other Illusions: Photographs of Indians by Edward S. Curtis* (New York: Pantheon, 1982); Janet Walker, *Westerns: Films Through History* (New York: Routledge, 2001).

29. Led largely by Orvell, *The Real Thing.*

30. Orvell, *The Real Thing*, xvii.

31. Daniel Boorstin, *The Image: A Guide to Pseudo-Events in America* (New York: Harper & Row, 1962).

32. Kurt Andersen, *Fantasyland: How America Went Haywire: A 500-Year History* (New York: Random House, 2017).

33. Andersen, *Fantasyland*, 4.

34. Andersen, *Fantasyland.*

35. Max Read, "How Much of the Internet Is Fake? It Turns Out, A Lot of It, Actually," *Intelligencer*, December 26, 2018, https://nymag.com/intelligencer/2018/12/how-much-of-the-internet-is-fake.html (accessed December 30, 2018).

36. Chronis is a professor of marketing at California State University at Stanislaus. Hampton is an emeritus professor of marketing at the University of Nebraska at Lincoln.

37. Athinodoros Chronis and Ronald D. Hampton, "Consuming the Authentic Gettysburg: How a *Touris* Landscape Becomes an Authentic Experience," *Journal of Consumer Behaviour* 7 (2008): 111-26; and Chronis, "Between Place and Story: Gettysburg as Tourism Imaginary," *Annals of Tourism Research* 36, no. 4 (2012): 1797-816. These authors are careful to note that (and cite) a significant body of literature on which their theories build. They do not claim to originate all of the theory presented, but they do make a reasonable claim for organizing the scholarship into a set of theoretical principles. See the two papers, especially the beginning section of each paper, for a useful literature review, which we do not take space to provide here.

38. Chronis and Hampton "Consuming the Authentic Gettysburg," 118.

39. Chronis, "Between Place and Story," 1797.

40. Chronis, "Between Place and Story," 1798.

41. Chronis, "Between Place and Story," 1807-8.

42. Chronis, "Between Place and Story," 1808.
43. Chronis, "Between Place and Story," 1808.
44. Chronis, "Between Place and Story," 1809.
45. Chronis, "Between Place and Story," 1809.
46. Chronis, "Between Place and Story," 1797.
47. Chronis, "Between Place and Story," 1809.

2

ACADEMIC RESEARCH BY TOURISM AND INFORMATION SCHOLARS

There are so many disciplines delving into tourism research that researchers in the field of tourism do not have the ability to build a unifying paradigm.[1]

AUTHENTICITY IN TOURISM SCHOLARSHIP

As academic interest in tourism increased in the 1970s and 1980s, scholars wanted to create a community of like-minded colleagues, behaving like other academic cohorts such as historians, sociologists, or economists. One milestone in the creation of an academic community is the establishment of peer-reviewed scholarly journals, which are used to channel research, debate issues associated with research agendas, create and refine theories, and introduce new specialized terminology. To better understand the process by which tourism scholars have created a discipline and studied the concept of authenticity, we have surveyed what went on within the pages of a single leading academic journal of tourism studies, the *Annals of Tourism Research.*[2]

This journal is particularly useful inasmuch as it began publishing in 1973, at the dawn of what is now a rapidly growing community of tourism scholars, who joined from various academic disciplines. Over the decades, the journal has covered a wide variety of topics—revealing that the intellectual scope of tourism studies has remained broadly conceived and that its boundaries have yet to be fixed. Papers in this journal began to address authenticity at the start of the 1980s. Interest in this topic surged from the late 1980s through mid-1990s, and then resurfaced as an interest in the 2000s. We identified 20 articles directly focused on the topic of authenticity, and dozens of other articles that address authenticity either in part or indirectly. As our discussion proceeds below, we typically identify the disciplines from which these authors came because the normative worldviews and techniques from their parent discipline are typically applied in their work on tourism.

We discuss three overarching themes that appeared in the first half century of publications in *Annals of Tourism Research*. One concerns understanding; it addresses the tension that exists between factual understanding of, say, a community's history and the desire to promote an altered, perhaps more positive image or story for economic or other reasons. A second theme concerns presentation, namely the tensions surrounding efforts by a community to serve up "educational" experiences in a truthful (authentic) manner. The third theme concerns changes that have come through the widespread use of the Internet, in particular its use by tourists and others to discuss their personal cultural tourism experiences and the authenticity of these experiences; these changes have multiplied many-fold the number of voices heard in these discussions.

In the following paragraphs, we discuss these three themes. After discussing the first two, we introduce an interlude—building on the first two themes—to explain why tourism scholars consider the topic of authenticity worthy of discussion and research. Then, after introducing the third theme, we consider the paths that tourism scholars have taken to build their studies into an academically rigorous discipline that enables them to analyze the notions of authenticity and its appropriation in ways that are empirically faithful to their observations of tourists, while at the same time having a conceptual and theoretical underpinning. This pattern in the growth of tourism studies is not unlike the search for discipline that has happened in information studies and other emerging academic fields of study.

Theme 1: Authenticity, Fake News, and Limits to Truth

Early discussions in the journal did not use the word "authenticity." However, the concern about this concept was apparent for decades before the term came into vogue—especially in various papers about business motivations to exploit cultural values and behaviors. One early influential scholar of this issue, the sociologist John Forster, introduced the term "phony folk-culture" in 1964; it was still in use in the 1980s.[3] Case studies of the effects of tourism on communities conducted in the 1970s and 1980s discussed, for example, the effects summer vacationers had upon a rural community with respect to local culture and self-perceptions of local residents. In one paper, for example, the anthropologist D. J. Greenwood, studying a northern Vermont community, framed his discussion in terms of mismatches between local "traditional values" (rooted in historical experiences and established long before tourists discovered the area) and the expectations of the tourists themselves as to what they would expect of life in northern Vermont. (Where are all those charming characters in their red plaid jackets? they wondered.) These tensions at times caused local norms to be altered to conform with these outsider expectations, resulting in the creation of a "phony-folk culture."[4]

Greenwood noted the impact these mismatches had: "The development of the phony-folk culture in Vermont is disruptive to traditional values," resulting in the locals "strip-mining their culture, both material and non-material, in order to sell it to outsiders."[5] As another scholar (archeologist J. W. Jordan) noted, this development alarmed local residents because it diluted "traditional community ideology," while the demands of tourists to provide them with a "traditional life" experience exceeded the capabilities of their town to provide this, forcing the locals "to commoditize their culture to meet demand."[6] Greenwood links authenticity to local identity in the face of real-life business activities. This set of contradictions and tensions has remained a theme in studies of tourism for nearly a half century.

By 1995, the word "authenticity" appeared more frequently in the journal, often bluntly as reflected in such a title as "Authenticity in Tourism," written by the geographer George Hughes, who also had experience in creating governmental tourist development plans.[7] During the 1970s and 1980s, various facets of authenticity were discussed in the journal.[8] Through two case studies, Hughes explored how "authentic" Scottish food was defined and how globalization trends in standardization of food shaped perceived authentic offerings in local settings. Local Scottish foodies faced participants in the tourist industry who factored additional considerations into what was considered authentic Scottish food, including the role of profit and national tourist economic development strategies. Hughes argued that the "social construction of authenticity is merely one manifestation of a larger thesis," involving the transformation of the definition of authenticity.[9] By the 1990s, scholars were paying attention to theories of large-scale social constructions such as economic globalization, and how tourism fit into those.[10] Hughes summarized the effects on authenticity: "There is a discernible anxiety, in some of this, about the duality of standards in which residents, and even tourists, can retain a belief in one thing (the 'authentic') while 'merely' presenting another to tourists (the 'staged'). Poststructuralist reading suggests that no such dual is possible and that touristic initiatives are 'real' changes."[11] What happens is that illusion wins out and "reality distinction collapses";[12] and yet myths rooted in territory remained and affected the local community. Hughes argued that local authenticity was under siege from commercial, globally based consumer consumption.

For students of information, that is a process driven by whatever "facts" or "misinformation" are recruited to the process. In Hughes's food studies, once developers of tourist promotions became involved, they appropriated the histories of Scottish foods and adorned them with exaggerations, for example, that a member of a royal family had introduced a particular original recipe centuries ago.[13] In an ironic turn of event, these developers used fake authenticity to create and energize a heritage. (We see shades of Lettice at work here.) Diluting preexisting "symbolic content of all cultural life on which it [authenticity] relied" changed its definition.[14] Authenticity commingled with globalization, blurring historical usage with misinformation. Hughes concludes by discussing the "retheorizing of authenticity," arguing that "the authenticity of a tourism artifact needs to be considered against a complex global picture of homogenizing and differentiating forces. Its ideological significance needs to be vested in an artifact."[15]

By the beginning of the twenty-first century, the argument was made that one had to create a sense of authenticity to improve tourism; it was a means to distance tourists from their normal existence. In other words, authenticity "is the respectable child of old-fashioned exoticism."[16] Writing in 2001 from an anthropological perspective, John P. Taylor signaled the field had sufficiently expanded that "there are at least as many definitions of authenticity as there are those who write about it"; that it has become a "philosopher's stone" providing a "dialectic between object and subject," between the "then and now."[17] Taylor advocated greater attention to ethnographic studies to shape definitions, and called for consideration of the role of "sincerity" (he calls the word a "philosophical cousin" of authenticity) that would lead to a shift in "moral perspectives" largely away from whatever locates tourism's value in the reproduction of objects and experiences, toward a form of tourism that communicates values deemed important to the providers of these experiences.[18] The record of the past is the model upon which reproductions of the past should be built, he argues.

For the scholar interested in information's truth, we find Hughes to offer a useful approach. He extends the now four-decades-long discussion of authenticity as something local versus what the tourism providers offer and the tourists want. Therein lay the gaps, which in the idiom of the information scholar is the fuzzy territory between truth and misinformation. Tourism scholars were thinking more of the differences between claimed truth and the need for reconstructed "facts" to facilitate tourism, while not abandoning completely the historical realities being recreated.

Various tourism scholars documented cases to demonstrate authenticity's forms—providing multiple specific examples of the concepts at work. As time passed, tourism scholars began to shape some of their discussion around the role of *staged authenticity*.[19] These discussions often focused on how these places or events should be reenacted or restaged—with perceived authenticity as a desired characteristic. Staging those events involved identifying what constituted authenticity. Was it about authentic locality—that is, where an historical event occurred or a scenario that gave a community a sense of its identity? Or was it a creation, say, of how an ethnic group lived in the 1800s? Or of what the local historical society worked out with their community's Chamber of Commerce or tourist promotion office? In 2003, two scholars cited the very existence of an old building itself as an example of a truthful, authentic "manifestation of heritage."[20] To heritage buildings and sites were often added recreation of rituals and dress, then further augmented by festivals (not of an historic origin, but instead creations of the twentieth- and twenty-first-century tourist eras). All these activities paid homage to some notion of "original." These various activities pandered to a desire for nostalgia, which it satisfied by presenting a representation of the historical past in a way consistent with the expectations of today's residents or tourists.

Again, the debate for scholars of tourism is how to bridge the gap between the realities of the past and today's simulated replica (often bowdlerized to remove much of the ugliness, such as the treatment of Blacks or Native Americans in the nineteenth century). This process, however, misinforms the public by creating an idealized image of traditions. Tourism scholars have documented that activity in which the inventors of the tourism experience equivocate between what a professional historian would report happened and what locals want to believe or think happened. The discourse quickly leads to an activity of reproduction, and in that process, traditions are created and changed over time. In the act of staging events, tourists and the event organizers exchange information about what each thinks they know or messages they wish to promulgate. Surveys of tourists' *aspiration* for historical experiences are explicit: food, dancing, learning about local history, observing locally applied skills, and acquiring mementos—all in a way that is regarded as authentic.[21] Thus, the definition of authenticity and the judgment as to the degree an experience is deemed authentic is decided by the media, local promoters, and tourists (and not by the history itself, or by the interpretations of disinterested expert historians).[22] The goal of the re-creation—the tourism scholars moreover argue—is also dependent in part on the demographics of the tourists. Older, more affluent people, for example, are more attracted to this kind of authentic tourist event than other age groups, and this audience applies its values and experience when rendering judgment on historical authenticity. This behavior seems to apply in most societies, not just in these sites in American towns.[23]

By 2018, tourism scholars had assimilated some of the terminology and ways of thinking evident in media and information studies, for example, using the phrase "fake news" and pondering the implications of this phenomena for the future study of authenticity and tourism in general. This is not surprising, given the essential role that information plays in the success of the tourist industry. Fake news can affect opinions, expectations, and behaviors of tourists. Fake news can affect the success of tourist providers. In 2019, the *Annals of Tourism Research* decided it needed to inquire about how other disciplines are handling fake news.[24] After offering a nominal definition of fake news, and acknowledging the role of President Donald Trump and the widespread availability of Internet access (a point discussed more fully below), the journal presented several examples of the use of fake news in tourist initiatives—in order to remind readers that they and employees in the industry were not immune from its effects. The central point was that "the lack of research [on fake news] with references to the tourism sector offers the opportunity for a challenging and fresh field of research."[25] The journal then suggested several specific topics worthy of special attention: ethics in media and journalism domains, marketing of tourism organizations, impact on tourists' perceptions and behaviors, and ways for tourist organizations to protect themselves, which might involve both regulatory and cybersecurity issues. The journal argued that prior work on authenticity by tourism scholars was a possible pathway to connect researchers to fake news investigations—and offered a bibliography that would be familiar to information scholars, but not necessarily to tourist industry scholars.[26]

The questions raised in these discussions in the journal in 2019 were primarily oriented toward tourism operations management, such as "Should fake news be permitted as accepted practice in tourism marketing?" or "To what extent are tourism information users aware of the existence and consequences of fake news?" The journal also raised questions about how a heritage site might protect itself from fake news, and how cybersecurity or terrorism mitigation fit into this consideration. The link to information studies reflected in the journal here is limited to these discussions about authenticity, even though there are many other ways in which information is important to tourism and tourism management. So far, we have focused on fake news and misinformation as a general element in tourism studies. We turn next to efforts to create an authentic heritage experience, and the roles that space, place, and culture play in these efforts.

Theme 2: Space, Place, and Culture in an Authentic Heritage Experience for Tourists

Our next theme concerns two notions appearing in hundreds of articles and books on tourism: first, whether the industry's activities appeal to tourists, especially ones who aspire to historical, educational heritage experiences; and second, how best to conceptualize the notion of authenticity. This line of scholarship focuses primarily on issues of space, place, and culture. The focus for tourism scholars here is on the physical nature of authenticity, disconnected mostly from epistemological or intellectual concerns. For example, in one line of literature that lasted through the 1980s, scholars were concerned about how American Indians viewed tourists and what they had to do to attract visitors to their homelands—with particular attention to how the tourist industry manipulated stereotypes. For these scholars, truth and authenticity are seen as manipulative activities warranting study—ones that introduce biases in what information is communicated between tourists and by the tourist industry. Folklorists joined in these discussions.[27] This particular example was an uneven exercise, because Anglo-American perspectives were heard more often than Indian perspectives.[28] Over time, these scholars came to the conclusion that authenticity is socially constructed.[29]

This line of research continued until the end of the twentieth century, by which time several new concepts had emerged. For instance, the literature discussed "object-related authenticity in tourism," which focuses on items, buildings, and tourist experiences; "constructive authenticity," which focuses on the form of authenticity actively projected onto what a tourist sees or experiences; and the "activity-related authenticity in tourism," which concerns the experiences of tourists. Discussions about the flow of information and how it is presented, regarding objects and activities, permeated the scholarly discourse. These discussions also mirrored ones taking place in several other academic disciplines about constructivism, modernism, and postmodernism.[30] For example, for those advocating constructivist approaches to authenticity and the roles of tourists, objects, and places, tourists are presented as seeking out symbolic authenticity—the result of social construction—as opposed to actual authenticity.[31] Ontological concepts drawn from speculative philosophy (in particular, Kierkegaard, Nietzsche, Sartre, and Camus) regarding existential experiences have appeared in this tourism literature since the 1970s.[32] Using various methodological approaches, tourism scholars raised questions about what tourists were thinking and wanted—and sometimes questioned the beliefs of both the tourists and the locals themselves. The nature of authenticity became a changing rather than a fixed concept for them.

Today, the pattern of discussing authenticity in tourism from both philosophical and practical perspectives is well established. The literature now includes a multiplicity of perspectives, and authors are expected to embed their work in a growing body of literature.[33] The theme of place, space, and experiences is deeply embedded in contentious discussions about theoretical constructs of tourism and its practices. As scholars in the tourism field noted recently, even the definition of authenticity "remains conceptually contested and has taken few steps towards becoming an 'anchor' for a tourism paradigm."[34] It is within this context that debates have occurred about the ontological status of objects, as performance or experience.

Some recent scholarship, importantly, has moved away from the authenticity of objects to the process by which objects or sites are authenticated. A distinction has recently emerged under the names "cool" and "hot" authentication (discussed further at the end of this chapter). *Cool authentication* is about emotionally detached, rationally established processes to identify the authenticity of objects and places. Scientists, historians, and other experts are recognized as establishing certification of an object or place. *Hot authentication* is about personal, emotionally based recognition of objects as authentic. It arises from performative, often emotionally charged acts related to tourists' experiences and beliefs, including the performance of rituals.[35] Both notions (cool, hot) are deeply rooted in heritage and cultural studies.[36] The distinctions between cool and hot authentication roughly parallel the differences between rational and speculative ways of knowing.

Interlude: Authenticity as a Topic Worthy of Discussion by Scholars

One might wonder why tourism scholars have devoted so much attention to the subject of authenticity. In the early tourism scholarship, authenticity was about the inherent properties of the product being presented to the tourist. But later, scholars questioned whether the authenticity rested in these inherent properties.[37] By 2010, the subject had been so extensively discussed that some tourism scholars argued that it was "a spent issue," irrelevant to the tourist who wanted novelty, or even a Disneyland perspective on history. Given the heightened worldwide sensitivity to fake facts and misinformation arising from the study of political discourse since 2015, there is increasing belief that either authenticity is not an objective fact, or at least the discussion of why people believe things to be authentic is as important or more important than objective authenticity. Some scholars argue that authenticity is a locally defined phenomenon, dependent on the attributes of a locality, or the needs, beliefs, experiences, and backgrounds of the tourists themselves. Some tourism scholars argue that this shows that tourism studies has not attained the solid foundations reached in other mature academic disciplines.[38] One expert has argued that "as long as tourists continue to concern themselves with evaluating authenticity or cultural objects and experiences by whatever criteria they apply, then authenticity should remain firmly embedded in the development of tourism theory."[39] That author was thinking like a business professional, clearly rooting this argument into the whole mission of the tourism industry; not like a scholar who is familiar with the social construction of knowledge and other postmodern notions.

Research methods borrowed from other business and academic disciplines are beginning to energize long-standing discussions among tourism scholars about authenticity. Marketing tools to understand customers, using a netnographic approach (i.e., online ethnography) are promising, especially given the willingness of tourists to engage scholars through surveys; and these tools provide a powerful quantitative tool to scholars.[40] This approach is providing significant amounts of data about the values, expectations, and experiences of tourists—all of which are invigorating scholarly debate about authenticity. For these scholars, the goal is a scientific one: through the collection and processing of additional contextual information to settle on and accept a canonical definition of authenticity that bears out this data.

Theme 3: Authenticity Based in Travel Stories on the Internet

The Internet has become a ready source of information for tourists.[41] It is used both as a marketing and communications tool for providers of tourist services, and for tourists to report on their experiences and to access information while they are visiting a heritage site.[42] Tourism scholars are still studying the implications of the Internet for authenticity in tourism.[43] One thing one can learn empirically from looking at travel websites is how cultural heritage providers are presenting themselves, as well as how this online information and communications affects the views and practices of tourists. Another topic ripe for study is how individuals and professional travel writers present their cultural heritage tourism experiences. How do they interpret what they found when they visited a site? How did their presentations relate to how it was portrayed by the provider? Which aspects were regarded as authentic, and why?

Certain websites and social networking sites—such as Facebook, Instagram, TripAdvisor, or Passion Passport—have been platforms where people regularly place information about tourism.[44] These different platforms have different technological affordances and they attract different audiences; and these differences are also ripe for study.[45] Articles posted on Facebook are being shaped differently from those on Instagram, thus "affecting their depiction of authenticity to fit these technological premises."[46] In these various online writings about tourism, both tourists and professional travel writers discuss their values and expectations of a touristic experience, but also often accentuate the differences between their experiences and those of others. Case studies suggest that, as in the long-standing paper travel guide literature, authors are continuing to differentiate their work from others—a topic of long interest to tourist scholars in understanding authenticity's truth versus misinformation.[47] So far, the *Annals of Tourism Research* has not addressed these issues in detail, from either a qualitative or quantitative standpoint.

DISCIPLINING TOURISM STUDIES WITH RESPECT TO AUTHENTICITY AND AUTHENTICATION

Tourism experts from around the world encounter each other in the pages of *Annals of Tourism Research*, where they craft theories and frameworks and discuss each other's ideas.[48] By the late 1980s, there was growing recognition that, to understand authenticity, these scholars had to explore such themes as the nature of commoditization, staged authenticity, and the frustrations of tourists seeking authentic experiences. As one expert said, "Authenticity is conceived as a negotiable rather than primitive concept," with the rigor of any definition shaped by its aspirational features across the three themes just mentioned.[49] Early elements of a theory-based definition posited that tourism leads to commoditization, which destroys the authenticity of "local cultural products and human relations"; while staged authenticity supplants the genuine desire of tourists for an authentic experience.[50] As a negotiated experience, tourists increasingly influenced scholarship in this area. Unlike cultural anthropology or sociology, tourism research has had a strong practice-oriented component and the tourism scholars have not been able to rely solely upon purely intellectual or research-based observations, but also have had to take into consideration the comments of tourists and managers in the tourism business.[51] This is most apparent in the commoditization discussions: tourism was regarded as a form of trade, of commercialization, and it thus came to be evaluated in terms of the selling and buying of experiences. As Erik Cohen observed in 1988, "Tourist-oriented products frequently acquire new meanings for the locals," even though older local means do not disappear completely.[52]

A quarter of a century later, the same social anthropologist, Erik Cohen, appropriated the concept of "hot" and "cool" authentication (from another tourism colleague who had introduced these concepts) in order to advance tourism theory.[53] Let us explore these notions in greater detail than we did above. Cohen (together with his co-author Scott Cohen) argued that the study of authenticity should be studied as a process of authentication, by which one "confirms" that an artifact, idea, or ritual is "original." He contrasted two common ways in which authentication takes place in the everyday world. One is *cool authentication*, in which the scientist or expert objectively declares an artifact or a site to be authentic; whereas *hot authentication* is based on the subjective experience of an individual who believes an artifact or site to be authentic. Table 2.1 provides a list of the characteristics of hot and cool authentication.

Here one sees a major step toward a theory of how authenticity can be defined and how it functions as both concept and action. Earlier scholarship had provided a series of scholarly case studies, which any new theory must provide an effective way of handling. The work of the Cohens admits these two different types of authentication, which most of these earlier case studies fell under. One type (cool) describes the process that goes on, for example, when the Smithsonian Institution certifies a site or museum, or an expert on Civil War history visits and proclaims the artifacts and the interpretation as, respectively, authentic and true. The other type (hot) describes the process of the individual Civil War buff gaining succor from their personal visit to a battlefield or participating in a battle reenactment. The Cohens note the possibility and even likelihood of multiple—potentially conflicting—instances and meanings of authentication of a single cultural historic site. Their research represents a turn from a description or analysis of the tourists' experiences to a more sociological explanation of the process by which a tourist accomplishes an experience they regard as authentic. These new ideas began to attract interest from scholars around the world.

Table 2.1   Cohens' Paradigm for Distinguishing Cool and Hot Authentication

Criterion	Cool Authentication	Hot Authentication
Basis of authority	Scientific knowledge claims, expertise, proof	Belief, commitment, devotion
Agent	Authorized person or institutions	No single identifiable agent, performative conduct of attending public
Approach	Formal criteria, accepted procedures	Diffuse and incremental
Role of public	Low, observer	High, imbricated, participatory
Practices	Declaration, certification, authentication	Ritual, offerings, communal support, resistance
Temporality	Single act, static	Gradual, dynamic, accumulative
Conducive to personal experiences	Objective authenticity	Existential authenticity
Continuance	Dependent on credibility of agent	Reiterative, requires continual (re)enactment
Impact on dynamics of attraction	Stagnating effect, fossilization	Augmentative and transformative

Source: Erik Cohen and Scott A. Cohen, "Authentication: Hot and Cool," *Annals of Tourism Research* 39, no. 3 (2012): 1303.

Cohen was in Israel, his co-author in England, while new discussions of his ideas came from yet other places, such as Australia.[54] It also led to discussion of tourism sites that are located far beyond the English-speaking world.

Because of the diverse backgrounds of tourism scholars discussing authenticity, it was inevitable that, from the 1960s to the present, they would bring into their debates the intellectual perspective of their various parent disciplines. One place this happened was in the role of knowledge. The aspiration of those teeing up discussions of "knowledge" (the word they used instead of "information") was to develop and understand a model of what constituted the tourism knowledge system. These concepts are still today being introduced to the larger community of tourism scholars as the field of tourism studies continues to develop methods and collect information that will help bring maturation to their field.[55] This process is requiring these scholars to extend the interdisciplinarity of their work, drawing upon other disciplines, including geography, sociology, law, economics, and psychology.[56] Understanding of the Web had to be included in this knowledge ecosystem as well.

Increasingly added to the authenticity conversation was "indigenous knowledge," information originating from local cultural and historical realities, for example, what Native American Indians believed and did.[57] It is here that discussions about postcolonial perspective have come especially into play.[58]

Tourism scholars came to realize that knowledge systems would have to be based on a wider net cast based on critique, synthesis, and continual revision of concepts. Thus, the discussions turned increasingly to such topics as epistemology, ontology, role of power and networks, systems thinking, and knowledge management within the tourist industry. How to conduct this kind of research animated many discussions.[59] As two tourist scholars observed, "all of these philosophical streams thus grapple with the qualitative gap between truth (or laws) and empirical reality."[60] These debates and issues continue to be discussed, but more from the perspective of social scientists and humanities scholars, such as phenomenology and science and technology studies.[61]

WHAT INFORMATION STUDIES HAS TO SAY ABOUT MISINFORMATION

To establish a basis of comparison between tourism studies and information studies, we examined library and information science journals for their coverage of misinformation in the years 2016 to 2021. We chose our starting date because of the growing attention to misinformation that resulted from the 2016 US presidential election and the campaign leading up to it. The journals were mostly chosen because they were in the top fifty in the SJR Scimago Journal Rankings on Library and Information Sciences and because the authors believed these journals might be venues for publications on misinformation.

We found relevant articles in *Information, Communication & Society*; *Library and Information Science Research*; *Information Processing & Management*; the *Journal of Documentation*; the *Proceedings of the Association for Information Science and Technology*; and the *Journal of the Association for Information Science and Technology*. From this top fifty list, we also examined *Information and Organization*; *College and Research Libraries*; and *Information Technology & People* but did not find relevant articles in any of them. We also surveyed two journals not ranked in the top fifty but which we thought might contain relevant articles: *Information & Culture* and *The Information Society*. However, they did not contain relevant articles, except for one written by one of the authors of this paper.[62] While we did not review the entirety of the more than two hundred library and information science journals ranked by SJR Scimago, we believe that our sample is representative of the coverage of misinformation in information studies journals. Given how much talk we hear about misinformation, both publicly and among our information studies colleagues, we were surprised by the small number of articles we found.

We found twenty-six articles, which represents approximately 1 percent of the publications we surveyed. For the most part, each of the journals that we surveyed presented a single approach to misinformation. For example, the journal *Library and Information Research* focused on the roles that libraries play in educating the public—and youth in particular—about misinformation.[63] Libraries have long played this public-facing educational role and are regarded as one of the leading types of public information institutions, together with museums and archives. Perhaps if we had surveyed the museum literature, we would have found articles about the role of museums in combatting misinformation.

A more recent development in information studies has been to introduce computational methods, such as natural language processing and machine learning. *Information Processing & Management* has published a number of articles on misinformation using this approach, and we also found a few articles using these methods in the proceedings and journal of the main information science professional society (ASIS&T) and elsewhere. Some of these articles continue a line of research on sentiment analysis and other affective issues, as applied to misinformation.[64] Other articles used these methods for various other topics.[65]

Both communication studies and media studies have grown closer to, and influenced, information studies over the past twenty years, especially because of the interests of all these disciplines in the Internet and social media. One sees this trend in particular in the misinformation articles that appear in the journal *Information, Communication & Society* but also in some of the other journals we surveyed.[66]

Several of the papers we found were intended to theorize the nature of misinformation.[67] The *Journal of Documentation* is regarded as information studies' leading journal of theory, and most of the papers cited in the notes in this section from that journal have a theory orientation to them.

No doubt driven in part by the 2016 American elections, the two topics related to misinformation that are most heavily studied by scholars from a variety of academic disciplines are fake news and misinformation in political discourse. Both of these topics are heavily represented in the survey that we conducted. We found a number of articles about fake news in both print and online media, including several papers theorizing about the topic, and ranging from information literacy to machine learning approaches.[68] Similarly, there were a number of papers on politics, including some about theory and another focusing on information behavior, which is a well-established subdiscipline within information studies.[69] In the case of both the fake news and political misinformation articles, most of the coverage was about the United States, but there were cases about other countries, including Scotland and Indonesia.

One other misinformation topic that received significant attention in these articles was health misinformation, especially online misinformation.[70] This is not surprising because information studies has a very active subdiscipline concentrating on health information.

CONNECTIONS BETWEEN AUTHENTICITY RESEARCH SCHOLARS AND MISINFORMATION RESEARCH SCHOLARS

In this section, we examine some of the connections between research on authenticity within tourism studies and on misinformation within information studies. But first, we speak of tourism studies and information studies more generally. While tourism is an information-rich activity, tourism studies has generally not focused explicitly on information issues other than some studies of tourism information management systems.[71] Thus, one might not expect to find much connection between these two academic disciplines.

While tourism studies and information studies may seem to be far removed from one another in content, there are nevertheless many similarities between the two fields. Cultural tourism is about imparting education to visitors—that is, about enabling them to gain knowledge (an information activity). Both fields study the role and functioning of museums. Concerns about cultural artifacts are at the heart of archival studies, a central subdiscipline of information studies. Information behavior, which once was focused on structured interaction between humans and formal information environments (such as research in a library or use of a computerized database), has moved far beyond these topics to examine everyday engagement with information such as through the use of the Internet or engagement with information while being a tourist at a cultural heritage site.

So far, when misinformation has been studied by information scholars, it has been discussed largely in terms of topical areas (e.g., information behavior, media studies) or research methods (e.g., computational methods, such as natural language processing and machine processing) that are already well established within information studies. In other words, misinformation is not so much a new domain of scholarship for information scholars—with its own concepts, frameworks, and methods—as it is an application of existing ways of thinking within information studies applied to a current topic. This suggests an opportunity for tourism studies to stimulate new ways of approaching misinformation (and perhaps even to revitalize subdisciplines of information studies beyond the study of misinformation).

One way in which tourism studies may be a stimulant to information studies is in broadening and rebalancing the interdisciplinary nature of information studies. It is too large a topic to take on this issue in generality, but in illustration consider the theories that are discussed in the well-known resource book, *Theories of Information Behavior*.[72] These theories are overwhelmingly drawn from psychology or sociology.[73] There is extensive application in tourism studies of concepts, research, and methods from the fields of economics, geography, and management information science; and these may provide exemplars for the information scholar. Another way in which tourism studies may be a stimulant to information studies is by its greater world perspective, both drawing on a set of scholars who are more dispersed around the globe than information studies scholars (who are predominantly in North America, Western Europe, and China), and by more often studying topics that are not sited in the English-speaking world.[74]

One other similarity between the tourism field and the library and information science field is the active participation of both practitioners (tourism managers, librarians) and scholarly theorists (based mostly in the academy). The ways in which practitioners set agendas, ground discussions in practical everyday activities, and interact with their more theoretical colleagues in the tourism studies discussions may provide insight to library and information science scholars.

Now let's turn to the connections between authenticity studies by tourism scholars and misinformation studies by information scholars. Tourism provides an excellent example of where an information environment is mediated by economic issues, and where these economic concerns often cause tensions over authenticity of artifacts and experience. There are only a few cases in information studies where economic considerations have been studied as an important factor, such as in the book industry and in Internet platforms; but it would be good to have additional examples in which economics is critical to information integrity.

One interesting feature of the tourism studies on authenticity is how important a consideration is place. There are areas in information studies where place is important, for example in the long-standing discussions of the design of library spaces and the experiential environment that they provide. These tourism studies that concern place sometimes speak of the impact of environment on various constituencies, for example on how changes to attract and accommodate tourists might affect the local population. This is not dissimilar from the discussions of libraries as places with multiple functions: that serve adult book patrons, children's basic enrichment education, and as social safety nets for the homeless or unemployed.

The small towns studied by tourism scholars, such as Lindsborg, Kansas (see chapter 3), are cultural heritage sites, just as are the museums and archival collections studied by information scholars. They face many of the same issues, such as intended audiences, roles in their local communities, augmentations of the formal education system for children, tensions between perceived traditional narratives and alternative narratives (sometimes involving underrepresented populations), tensions between the worship of the artifact and the focus on its interpretation, and questions over real versus staged authenticity.

Another similarity is that some of the action does not take place at the tourist site or in the library or bookstore, but instead online, involving both suppliers (tourism site managers, local economic development officers, travel writers, booksellers, authors) and consumers (tourists, locals, readers). Studies of the populations and writings on a travel site such as TripAdvisor would make interesting comparison to the populations and writings on a book site such as Goodreads.

In the last decade, there has been a common notion among tourism scholars of authenticity as socially constructed. In the information studies literature, the notion of social construction of knowledge is much older. For example, in 1952 the information scholars Margaret Egan and Jesse Shera introduced the concept of "social epistemology."[75] While the notion of social construction of knowledge is well known in sociological and philosophical circles, information scholars have not extensively discussed the social construction of misinformation. Perhaps scholars know or surmise the reasons why a politician presents a fake fact, but there has been little investigation of the process by which, for example, QAnon followers accept some falsehoods as truths, but not others. The tourism scholars are on to something by focusing on authentication, which is a process, rather than authenticity, which is simply a trait or characteristic. Reading the tourism scholarship about the social construction of authenticity may provide guidelines to information scholars. Similarly, the Cohens' research, described above, on studying the process of authentication as opposed to authenticity may provide information scholars with insights into belief in misinformation, as may their notions of hot (emotionally charged practices based on individual experiences and beliefs) and cool authentication (based in rationally established practices). Other notions of the tourism scholars, such as the concepts of object-related authenticity versus constructive authenticity, and activity-related authenticity can also readily be transferred over to the misinformation scholarship of information scholars.

NOTES

1. Justin M. A. Taillon, "Understanding Tourism as an Academic Community, Study, or Discipline," *Journal of Tourism & Hospitality* 3, no. 3 (2014), https://www.academia.edu/9780382/Tourism_as_an_academic _discipline.

2. We have examined every issue of *Annals of Tourism Research*. We have also examined the *International Journal of Tourism Research*, but less extensively and less systematically.

3. John Forster, "The Sociological Consequences of Tourism," *International Journal of Comparative Sociology* 5 (January 1964): 217–27.

4. Davydd J. Greenwood, "Culture by the Pound: An Anthropological Perspective of Tourism as Cultural Commoditization," in *Hosts and Guests: The Anthropology of Tourism*, edited by V. L. Smith, 129–38 (Philadelphia: University of Pennsylvania Press, 1977).

5. Greenwood "Culture by the Pound."

6. James William Jordan, "The Summer People and the Natives: Some Effects of Tourism in a Vermont Vacation Village," *Annals of Tourism Research* 7, no. 1 (1980): first quote 50, others 53.

7. George Hughes, "Authenticity in Tourism," *Annals of Tourism Research* 22, no. 4 (1995): 781–803.

8. L. Boynton, "The Effect of Tourism on Amish Quilting Design," *Annals of Tourism Research* 13 (1986): 451–65; E. Cohen, "Authenticity and Commoditization in Tourism," *Annals of Tourism Research* 15 (1988): 371–86; D. MacCannell, "Staged Authenticity: Arrangements of Social Space in Tourist Settings," *American Journal of Sociology* 79 (1973): 589–603 also his, *The Tourist: A New Theory of the Leisure Class* (New York: Schocken, 1976); P. L. Pearce and G. M. Moscardo, "The Concept of Authenticity in Tourist Experiences," *Australian and New Zealand Journal of Sociology* 22 (1986): 121–32.

9. Hughes, "Authenticity in Tourism," 782.

10. P. Boniface and P. J. Fowler, *Heritage and Tourism in the Global Village* (London: Routledge, 1993); A. Poon, *Tourism, Technology and Competitive Strategies* (Wallingford: CAB International, 1993); U. Wagner, "Out of Time and Place: Mass Tourism and Charter Trips," *Ethnos* 42 (1977): 38–52.

11. On the shaping of post-disciplinary thought for tourism studies, John Tribe and Janne J. Liburd, "The Tourism Knowledge System" (*Annals of Tourism Research* 57 [2016]: 44–61) points the reader to A. Sayer, "Long Live Postdisciplinary Studies! Sociology and the Curse of Disciplinary Parochialism/ Imperialism" (Lancaster Department of Sociology, Lancaster University, 1999). On an effort to heal the destructive tendencies of post-disciplinary thought in tourism studies, see Brendan Canavan and Claire McCamley, "Negotiating Authenticity: Three Modernities," *Annals of Tourism Research* 88 (2021); and Elizabeth S. Vidon, Jillian M. Rickly, and Daniel Knudsen, "Wilderness State of Mind: Expanding Authenticity," *Annals of Tourism Research* 73 (2018): 62–70.

12. Hughes, "Authenticity in Tourism," 784.

13. Hughes, "Authenticity in Tourism," 786.

14. Hughes, "Authenticity in Tourism," 790.

15. Hughes, "Authenticity in Tourism," 799.

16. S. Rushdie, *Imaginary Homelands: Essays and Criticism, 1981–1991* (London: Granta, 1991): 67.

17. John P. Taylor, "Authenticity and Sincerity in Tourism," *Annals of Tourism Research*, 28, no. 1 (2001): 8, full article, 7–26.

18. Taylor, "Authenticity and Sincerity in Tourism," 8–9.

19. The concept of staged authenticity was introduced by D. MacCannell, "Staged Authenticity: Arrangements of Social Space in Visitor Settings," *American Journal of Sociology* 79, no. 3 (1979): 589–603. Deepak Chhabra, Robert G. Healy, and Erin Sills, "Staged Authenticity and Heritage Tourism," *Annals of Tourism Research* 30, no. 3 (2003): 702–19 argue that "high perception of

authenticity can be achieved even when the event is staged in a place far away from the original source of the cultural tradition" (702). See also M. Balcar and D. Pearce, *Heritage Tourism on the West Coast of New Zealand* (no city: Tourism Management, 1996); A. Fyall and B. Garrod, "Heritage Tourism: At What Price?" *Managing Leisure* 3 (1998): 213–28; D. Herbert, "Literary Places, Tourism and the Heritage Experience," *Annals of Tourism Research* 28 (2001): 319–33; Y. Poria, R. Butler, and D. Airey, "Clarifying Heritage Tourism," *Annals of Tourism Research* 28 (2001): 1047–49.

20. Chhabra, Healy, and Sills, "Staged Authenticity and Heritage Tourism," 704.

21. Chhabra, Healy, and Sills, "Staged Authenticity and Heritage Tourism," 702–19.

22. For example, Chhabra, Healy, and Sills, "Staged Authenticity and Heritage Tourism," 715–16.

23. Chhabra, Healy, and Sills, "Staged Authenticity and Heritage Tourism," 716.

24. Giancarlo Fedeli, "'Fake News' Meets Tourism: A Proposed Research Agenda," *Annals of Tourism Research* 80 (2020): 102684, https://www.research-gate.net/publication/328540173_'Fake_news'_meets_Tourism_a_proposed_research_agenda.

25. Fedeli, "'Fake News' Meets Tourism," 2.

26. This was not the first effort to compare discussions within a tourism journal, suggesting that tourism scholars were interested in borrowing from other disciplines approaches and issues to examine. For instance, see Haywantee Ramkissoon, Robin Nunkoo, and Stephen L. J. Smith, "Residents' Attitudes to Tourism: A Longitudinal Study of 140 Articles from 1984–2010," *Journal of Sustainable Tourism* 21, no. 1 (2012). They studied articles published in *Annals of Tourism Research, Tourism Management, and Travel Research.* They concluded that "although most articles were atheoretical, over the survey period an increasing proportion of studies made use of a variety of theories drawn from other disciplines to investigate the topic. The majority of studies were quantitative in nature, while a few studies used qualitative and mixed-methods approaches" and "that studies on the topic have evolved from being low on methodological sophistication and theoretical awareness to being high on both aspects," 5.

27. For example, Deirdre Evans-Pritchard, "How 'They See Us': Native American Images of Tourists," *Annals of Tourism Research* 16 (1989): 89–105.

28. For one example of sociological and folklore interest, see, C. Alberts and William R. James, "Tourism and the Changing Image of the Great Lakes Indians," *Annals of Tourism Research* 10 (1983): 123–48.

29. For example, using country and western American music as the discursive case study, see Richard A. Peterson, "In Search of Authenticity," *Journal of Management Studies* 42, no. 5 (July 2005): 1083–98.

30. For an excellent summary of the literature and arguments over the period 1960s–1990s, see Ning Wang, "Rethinking Authenticity in Tourism Experience," *Annals of Tourism Research*, 26, no. 7 (1999): 349–70. The author is a sociologist.

31. Wang, "Rethinking Authenticity in Tourism Experience," 356.

32. P. L. Berger and T. Luckmann, *The Social Construction of Reality: A Treatise in the Sociology of Knowledge* (Middlesex: Penguin, 1971); J. Golomb, *In Search of Authenticity* (London: Routledge, 1995).

33. Not surprisingly, then, one sees extensive citation in recent publications, as opposed to earlier papers in tourism studies which were pioneering new fields and cited fewer studies. See, for example, Brendan Canavan and Claire McCamley, "Negotiating Authenticity: Three Modernities," *Annals of Tourism Research* 88 (2021) preprint; and Kevin Moore, Annae Buchmann, Maria Mansson, and David Fisher, "Authenticity in Tourism and Experience. Practically Indispensable and Theoretically Mischievous?" *Annals of Tourism Research* 89 (2021): 1–11.

34. Moore et al., "Authenticity in Tourism and Experience," 1.

35. Erik Cohen and Scott A. Cohen, "Authentication: Hot and Cool," *Annals of Tourism Research* 39, no. 3 (2012): 1295–314.

36. Y. Reisinger and C. Steiner, "Reconceptualizing Object Authenticity," *Annals of Tourism Research*, no. 1 (2006): 65–86.

37. Muchazondida Mkono, "Authenticity Does Matter," *Annals of Tourism Research*, 39 no. 1 (2012): 480–83.

38. Mkono, "Authenticity Does Matter," 481.

39. Mkono, "Authenticity Does Matter."

40. R. V. Kozinets, "Netnography," in *Handbook of Qualitative Research Methods in Marketing*, edited by R. W. Belk (Cheltenham: Edward Elgar, 2006): 129–42.

41. Already, the evidence is accumulating that tourists are willing to describe online their experiences, what one would have called "travel writing," in earlier times. That older literature provided insights about what tourists and observers of tourism valued. See L. Pratt, *Imperial Eyes: Travel Writing and Transculturation* (London: Routledge, 1992).

42. On this last point, see Lídia Oliveira, *Handbook of Research on Digital Communications, Internet of Things, and the Future of Cultural Tourism* (Hershey: IGI Global, 2022).

43. Xavier Salet, "The Search for the Truest of Authorities: Online Travel Stories and Their Depiction of the Authentic in the Platform Economy," *Annals of Tourism Research* 88 (2021), preprint. On Passion Passport, Salet identifies certain themes that arise frequently in the travel writing: writer's connectivity with the place visited, differences in material wealth between the traveler and the indigenous population, feelings of privilege and guilt, and a search for the

spiritual. In a recent survey by the American Academy of Arts & Sciences, of twenty sources of historical information, museums and historic sites were the sources deemed most trustworthy, while social media was only ranked nineteenth of twenty sources in trustworthiness (with history-related video games the only less trustworthy source) (Burkholder and Schaffer 2021).

44. Salet, "The Search for the Truest of Authorities."

45. P. Lugosi," Socio-Technological Authenticity," *Annals of Tourism Research* 58 (2016): 100–13. Lugosi's research is framed in the sociologically based science and technologies study theory of actors and networks (ANT).

46. Salet, "The Search for the Truest of Authorities," 9.

47. Salet, "The Search for the Truest of Authorities."

48. These scholarly discussions also appear in other journals as well. See, Ramkissoon, Nunkoo, and Smith, "Residents' Attitudes to Tourism: A Longitudinal Study of 140 Articles from 1984–2010," 5–25.

49. Cohen, "Authenticity and Commoditization in Tourism," 371.

50. Cohen, "Authenticity and Commoditization in Tourism."

51. Richard Handler discussed similar issues at the same time in anthropology circles, "Authenticity," *Anthropology Today* 2, no. 1 (February 1986): 2–4.

52. Cohen, "Authenticity and Commoditization in Tourism," 383.

53. Cohen and Cohen, "Authentication: Hot and Cool," 1295–314.

54. Muchazondida Mkono, "Hot and Cool Authentication: A Netnographic Illustration," *Annals of Tourism Research* 41 (2013): 215–18.

55. Tribe and Liburd, "The Tourism Knowledge System." Tribe has written extensively on this theme; for his bibliography, see his 2016 article.

56. Some examples of works that move in these directions include: Jane Lovell and Chris Bull, *Authentic and Inauthentic Places in Tourism* (New York: Routledge, 2018); David Grazian, "Demystifying Authenticity in the Sociology of Culture," *Selected Works of David Grazian*, (Berkley, CA: BePress, 2010), https://works.bepress.com/david_grazian/12/ (accessed March 29, 2022); Deidre Evans-Pritchard, "The Portal Case: Authenticity, Tourism, Traditions, and the Law," *Journal of American Folklore* (1987); William R. Eadington and Milton Redman, "Economics and Tourism," *Annals of Tourism Research* 18, no. 1 (1991): 41–56; Philip L. Pearce and Jan Packer, "Minds on the Move: New Links from Psychology to Tourism," *Annals of Tourism Research* 40 (2013): 386–411; and Zhu, Yujie. *Heritage Tourism: From Problems to Possibilities* (Cambridge, UK: Cambridge University Press, 2021).

57. J. J. Liburd, "Tourism Research 2.0," *Annals of Tourism Research* 39, no. 2 (2012): 883–907.

58. D. Chambers and C. Buzinde, "Tourism and Decolonization: Locating Research and Self," *Annals of Tourism Research* 51 (2015): 1–16.

59. Juergen Gnoth and Ning Wang, "Authentic Knowledge and Empathy in Tourism," *Annals of Tourism Research* 50 (2015): 159–72; for original concepts,

D. MacCannell, *The Tourist: A New Theory of the Leisure Class* (New York: Schocken, 1976); Wang, "Rethinking Authenticity in Tourism Experience," 349–70; J. Gnoth and X. Matteucci, "A Phenomenological View of the Behavioral Tourism Research Literature," *International Journal of Culture, Tourism and Hospitality Research* 8, no. 1 (2014): 3–21.

60. Gnoth and Wang, "Authentic Knowledge and Empathy in Tourism," 159.

61. Peter Lugosi, "Socio-Technological Authentication," *Annals of Tourism Research* 58 (2016): 100–113, which includes a rich bibliography; J. J. Zhang, "Rethinking 'Heritage' in Post-Conflict Tourism," *Annals of Tourism Research* 66 (2017): 183–215; Vidon, Rickly, and Knudsen, "Wilderness State of Mind: Expanding Authenticity"; Moore et al., "Authenticity in Tourism and Experience. Practically Indispensable and Theoretically Mischievous?"

62. William Aspray, "Making and Debunking Myths About the Old West: A Case Study of Misinformation for Information Scholars," *Information & Culture* 56, no. 3 (2021): 251–78.

63. See, for example, M. Connor Sullivan, "Leveraging Library Trust to Combat Misinformation on Social Media," *Library & Information Science Research* 41, no. 1 (2019): 2–10; J. Buschman, "Good News, Bad News, and Fake News: Going Beyond Political Literacy to Democracy and Libraries," *Journal of Documentation* 75, no. 1 (2019): 213–28.

64. See, for example, Rina Kumari, Nischal Ashok, Tirthankar Ghosal, and Asif Ekbal, "What the Fake? Probing Misinformation Detection Standing on the Shoulder of Novelty and Emotion," *Information Processing & Management* 59, no. 1 (2022); Rina Kumari, Nischal Ashok, Tirthankar Ghosal, and Asif Ekbal, Misinformation detection using multitask learning with mutual learning for novelty detection and emotion recognition, *Information Processing & Management* 58, no. 5 (2021).

65. S. O. Soe (2018), "Algorithmic Detection of Misinformation and Disinformation: Gricean Perspectives," *Journal of Documentation* 74, no. 2 (2018): 309–32.

66. See, for example, Katja de Vries, "You Never Fake Alone. Creative AI in Action," *Information, Communication & Society* 23, no. 14 (2020): 2110–27; David C. DeAndrea, Stephanie Tom Tong, and Young-shin Lim, "What Causes More Mistrust: Profile Owners Deleting User-Generated Content or Website Contributors Masking their Identities," *Information, Communication & Society* 21, no. 8 (2018): 1068–80; Zongmin Li, Qi Zhang, Xinyu Du, Yanfang Ma, and Shihang Wang, "Social Media Rumor Refutation Effectiveness: Evaluation, Modelling and Enhancement," *Information Processing & Management* 58, no. 1 (2021); Rodrigo Barbado, Oscar Araque, and Carlos A. Iglesias, "A Framework for Fake Review Detection in Online Consumer Electronics Retailers," *Information Processing & Management* 56, no. 4 (2019); Pnina Fichman and Samantha

Sharp, "Successful Trolling on Reddit: A Comparison Across Subreddits in Entertainment, Health, Politics, and Religion," *Proceedings of the Association for Information Science and Technology* 10.1002/pra2.333, 57, no. 1 (2020). The Fichman and Sharp article is a content analysis of online posts on the relationship between misinformation and trolling; Fichman is an expert on the online behavior of trolling.

67. See, for example, Hilda Ruokolainen and Gunilla Widén, "Conceptualising Misinformation in the Context of Asylum Seekers," *Information Processing & Management* 57, no. 3 (2020).

68. See Junxiao Xue, Yabo Wang, Yichen Tian, Yafei Li, Lei Shi, and Lin Wei, "Detecting Fake News by Exploring the Consistency of Multimodal Data," *Information Processing & Management* 58, no. 5 (2021); Xichen Zhang and Ali A. Ghorbani, "An Overview of Online Fake News: Characterization, Detection, and Discussion," *Information Processing & Management* 57, no. 2 (2020); Vivek K. Singh, Isha Ghosh, and Darshan Sonagara, "Detecting Fake News Stories Via Multimodal Analysis," *Journal of the Association for Information Science and Technology* 72 (2021): 3–17; Andrew Duffy, Edson Tandoc, and Rich Ling, "Too Good to Be True, Too Good Not to Share: The Social Utility of Fake News," *Information, Communication & Society* 23, no. 13 (2020): 1965–79; Emily K. Vraga and Melissa Tully, "News Literacy, Social Media Behaviors, and Skepticism toward Information on Social Media," *Information, Communication & Society* 24, no. 2 (2021): 150–66; Febbie Austina Kwanda and Trisha T. C. Lin, "Fake News Practices in Indonesian Newsrooms During and After the Palu Earthquake: A Hierarchy-of-Influences Approach," *Information, Communication & Society* 23, no. 6 (2020): 849–66; Matt Carlson, "Fake News as an Informational Moral Panic: The Symbolic Deviancy of Social Media During the 2016 US Presidential Election," *Information, Communication & Society* 23, no. 3 (2020): 374–88; V. L. Rubin, "Disinformation and Misinformation Triangle: A Conceptual Model for 'Fake News' Epidemic, Causal Factors and Interventions," *Journal of Documentation* 75, no. 5 (2019): 1013–34.

69. See R. Marcella, G. Baxter, and A. Wallicka, "User Engagement with Political 'Facts' in the Context of the Fake News Phenomenon: An Exploration of Information Behaviour," *Journal of Documentation* 75, no. 5 (2019): 1082–99; G. Baxter, R. Marcella, and A. Wallicka, "Scottish Citizens' Perceptions of the Credibility of Online Political 'Facts' in the 'Fake News' Era: An Exploratory Study," *Journal of Documentation* 75, no. 5 (2019): 1100–23; Anupam Das and Ralph Schroeder, "Online Disinformation in the Run-Up to the Indian 2019 Election," *Information, Communication, & Society* 24, no. 12 (2021): 1762–78; and Gül Seçkin, Susan Hughes, Patricia Campbell, and Megan Lawson, "In Internet We Trust: Intersectionality of Distrust and Patient Non-Adherence," *Information, Communication, & Society* 24, no. 5 (2021): 751–71.

70. See Carlo Bianchini, Ivana Truccolo, Ettore Bidoli, and Mauro Mazzo-cut, "Avoiding Misleading Information: A Study of Complementary Medicine Online Information for Cancer Patients," *Library & Information Science Research* 41, no. 1 (2019): 67–77; Yuelin Li, Zhenjia Fan, Xiaojun Yuan, and Xiu Zhang, "Recognizing Fake Information through a Developed Feature Scheme: A User Study of Health Misinformation on Social Media in China," *Information Processing & Management* 59, no. 1 (2022); and Emily K. Vraga and Leticia Bode, "I Do Not Believe You: How Providing a Source Corrects Health Misperceptions across Social Media Platforms," *Information, Communication & Society* 21, no. 10 (2018): 1337–53.

71. See, for example, T. Bahaire and M. Elliott-White, "The Application of Geographical Information Systems (GIS) in Sustainable Tourism Planning: A Review," *Journal of Sustainable Tourism* 7, no. 2 (1999): 159–74; B. Pröll and W. Retschitzegger, Discovering Next Generation Tourism Information Systems: A Tour on TIScover," *Journal of Travel Research* 39, no. 2 (2000): 182–91; A. Maedche and S. Staab, "Applying Semantic Web Technologies for Tourism Information Systems," *ENTER* (January 2002): 311–19; B. Pröll, W. Retschitzegger, R. Wagner, and A. Ebner, "Beyond Traditional Tourism Information Systems: The Web-Based Approach TIScover," *Information Technology & Tourism* 1, no. 1 (1998): 15–31; and P. J. Sheldon, "Destination Information Systems," *Annals of Tourism Research* 20, no. 4 (1993): 633–49.

72. Karen E. Fisher, Sandra Erdelez, and Lynne McKechnie, *Theories of Information Behavior* (Medford, NJ: Information Today, 2005).

73. There are a few theories drawn from other fields: education (Big6 Skills for Information Literacy), ecology (Ecological Theory of Human Information Behavior), organizational studies (Information Activities in Work Tasks), anthropology (Institutional Ethnography), critical studies (Reader Response Theory), and feminist studies (Women's Ways of Knowing). However, these examples are small in number compared to those drawn from psychology or sociology.

74. It would take us too far afield, for example, to do an analysis of the home countries of authors in the leading tourism studies journals compared to the home countries of authors in the leading information studies journals, but our strong impression is that the tourism field has a more widely dispersed set of authors. One quick indicator is to take a look at the iSchools organization (see ischools.org). Of the thirty-eight information schools and departments that have the full (iCaucus) membership that enables them to sit on the governing board of the organization, twenty-two are in North America and ten are in China. One encouraging note is the number of schools and departments at all levels of membership has increased in recent years to 122, with thirty-four in the Asia/Pacific region, thirty-four in Europe, and fifty-four in North America—suggesting that participation in information studies is growing worldwide.

Perhaps the largest worldwide reach in the information studies field is through IFLA, the International Federation of Library Associations and Institutions. It was founded in 1927 with members from fifteen countries; and today it has members from 150 countries.

75. Margaret E. Egan and Jesse H. Shera, "Foundations of a Theory of Bibliography," *Library Quarterly* 22, no. 2 (1952). For an historical discussion of this development, see Jonathan Furner, "A Brilliant Mind": Margaret Egan and Social Epistemology," *Library Trends* 52 (2004).

3

AUTHENTICITY IN SMALL HERITAGE TOURISM SITES

The Case of Lindsborg, Kansas

This chapter investigates authenticity provided by small heritage sites. In 2007, the Small Museums Committee of the American Association for State and Local History (AASLH) defined a small museum to be one that has an annual budget under $250,000. Some of these small museums are much smaller than that. These small museums typically have no or very few paid employees, and they often survive primarily on the basis of volunteer labor. While they vary enormously in quality, it is often the case that the volunteers participate because of a love for their subject matter rather than professional training or experience in the principal areas covered by the museum. Collections and exhibits can be eclectic rather than coherent in these museums, for example, when a local history museum is reliant upon the donation of artifacts from various members of the local community. Running a museum involves a wide range of skills—ranging from finance, to public relations, to curatorial expertise—and many of these museums gain these skills catch as catch can, sometimes aided by outside professional organizations such as the AASLH. While some of these heritage sites offer an excellent experience and high-quality information to tourists, this category of small museums is the one most likely to be subject to providing misinformation. These small museums are also the ones most at risk of closing, with the death or diminished interest of founders or key volunteers, or because of an unsteady income or a natural disaster. For example, Ted's Old Iron Farm and Museum in Columbus, Kansas, a museum of old agricultural implements, closed in 2014 upon the death of the owner, Ted Hauser, at the age of eighty-two.[1]

Our case study in this chapter is about towns that build upon their ethnic heritage to become tourist destinations, and, in particular, about Lindsborg, Kansas, publicized as "Little Sweden, USA." Lindsborg is a small ethnic heritage site, but there are many other types of heritage sites that we could have just as easily written about here. To get a sense of the wide range of heritage sites, let us examine the list of museums in Kansas that appears in Wikipedia, which contains 343 entries and is likely to be incomplete. Table 3.1 provides an analysis of this list, counting the number of museums of each type and giving an example of such a museum and its location. Not all of the museums in this list are small. The largest cities (Wichita, Overland Park, Topeka) and the university towns (Emporia, Lawrence, Manhattan) are more likely to have larger museums; and there is the occasional smaller town with a large museum, such as the Eisenhower presidential library in the small

Table 3.1   Museums in Kansas

Type of museum	Number in Kansas	Example	Location of example
Local history	134	Anderson County Museum	Anderson
Art	30	Birger Sandzen Memorial Gallery	Lindsborg
Historic houses	26	Carrie Nation Home	Medicine Lodge
Open-air	22	McPherson County Old Mill Museum	Lindsborg
General history	21	They Also Ran Gallery	Norton
Science and technology (mostly automotive, aviation, railroad—not counting agriculture)	21	Iron Horse Museum	Parsons
Military	8	Frontier Army Museum	Fort Leavenworth
Ethnic, African American, or Native American	6	Roniger Memorial Museum	Cottonwood Falls
Agriculture	5	Yesteryear Museum	Salina

Source: "List of museums in Kansas," Wikipedia (accessed January 20, 2022). Some of the museums listed as general history may have been primarily local history museums. Types of museums with five or fewer of that type in Kansas include: amusement, biographical, cultural, doll, education, food, industry, medical, scouting, sports, and wax.

town of Abilene, Kansas (not to be confused with the much larger town of Abilene, Texas). Of the museums, 134 (39 percent) focus on local history, while thirty (9 percent) are art museums and twenty-six (8 percent) are historic houses. The other most common types can be seen in the table. The ethnic towns that we focus on in this chapter most commonly fall under local history or open-air museum categories.

THE SETTING OF ETHNIC HERITAGE TOURISM

Before turning to our case study about Lindsborg, let us be more specific about the places where this variety of ethnic heritage tourism occurs in the United States and what kinds of cultural artifacts are used to convey the heritage message.[2] Table 3.2 provides a sample, but by no means a complete list, of American towns that consciously set out to promote their ethnic or national heritage. We focus here on towns rather than cities in part because most people have historically lived outside of cities; and even in 2019, only 39 percent of the US population lived in places with more than fifty thousand people.[3] Another reason for focusing on towns is that in cities, where there are typically multiple ethnic groups and where interaction between these groups is easier, it is more difficult to see the full force of performance of a single ethnic identity.

Table 3.3 lists cultural artifacts associated with these heritage towns. Sometimes these cultural artifacts are historically accurate. But at other times, they are inauthentic in one way or another, perhaps for various reasons: memory of how things were done in the old country are lost or misremembered; materials are not available, or social and organizational structures are not conducive, to perfectly reproduce the way things were done "back home"; economic or social forces have established powerful new traditions in the new country; some new features of the way things were done in the old country do not fit so well with the mythological understanding of the old country, so new practices are intentionally adopted that fit better for the town's citizens with their own understanding of their ethnic identity; or city planners, tour guides (like Lettice, with whom we opened this book), or tourism marketing specialists change things to make them appear more in keeping with what the prospective tourist regards as authentic or interesting. Entertainment value—and sometimes potential revenue generation—is sometimes more important than authenticity, although authenticity is also important because of the goal of the tourist in gaining an education.

CHAPTER 3

Table 3.2 Small American Towns with a Strong National or Ethnic Identity

Czech	• Conway, North Dakota
	• West, Texas
	• Oak Creek, Nebraska
	• Wilber, Nebraska
	• Shiner, Texas
	• Montgomery, Minnesota
	• Lonsdale, Minnesota
	• Cedar Rapids, Iowa
Danish	• Solvang, California
	• Elk Horn, Iowa
	• Blair, Nebraska
	• Greenville, Michigan
	• Dannebrog, Nebraska
Dutch	• Pella, Iowa
	• Holland, Michigan
	• Zeeland, Michigan
	• Grand Rapids, Michigan
	• Orange City, Iowa
	• Rock Rapids, Iowa
	• Sioux City, Iowa
	• Fulton, Illinois
	• Celeryville, Illinois
	• Little Chute, Wisconsin
	• Lynden, Washington
	• Ripon, California
Finnish	• Cokato, Minnesota
	• New York Mills, Minnesota
	• Duluth, Minnesota
	• Calumet, Michigan
	• Hancock, Michigan
	• Marquette, Michigan
	• Ishpaming, Michigan
	• Negaunee, Michigan
	• Ironwood, Michigan
German	• Fredericksburg, Texas
	• New Braunfels, Texas
	• Brenham, Texas
	• Amana Colonies, Iowa
	• New Ulm, Minnesota
	• Leavenworth, Washington
Norwegian	• Stoughton, Wisconsin
	• Mt. Horeb, Wisconsin
	• Spring Grove, Minnesota
	• Decorah, Iowa
	• Moorhead, Minnesota
	• Westby, Wisconsin

(Continued)

Table 3.2 (Continued)

Scottish	• Franklin, North Carolina
	• Hocking Hills, Ohio
Swedish	• Lindsborg, Kansas
	• Lindstrom, Minnesota
	• Bishop Hill, Illinois
	• New Sweden, Maine
	• Stockholm, Maine
	• Scandia, Minnesota
	• Stockholm, Wisconsin
Swiss	• New Glarus, Wisconsin
	• Berne, Indiana
	• Monticello, Wisconsin
	• Highland, Illinois

Migration from Europe to the United States began in significant numbers in the 1830s, rose by a factor of four in the 1850s, doubled again in the 1870s, and was even greater in the final decades of the nineteenth century and in the first two decades of the twentieth century—then tapering off throughout the remainder of the twentieth century. There was migration from every country in Europe, but some countries sent more people to America than others. The Irish tended to settle in large cities such as Boston, New York, and Chicago. The Scots and Danes tended to be more dispersed than other nationalities, and they tended to assimilate more quickly than other groups. Czechs, the Dutch, Finns, Germans, Norwegians, Swedes, and the Swiss tended to congregate in rural small towns—often in upper New England, the Midwest, or Texas—where they constituted a majority or substantial minority of the population, and where some form of their culture predominated in town life.

Many of these people were handy and built their own buildings—initially in the style and with the methods that they had learned in the old country. They hungered for the specialty foods of their old country, and a local market

Table 3.3 Cultural Artifacts Affiliated with National or Ethnic Identity in Small US Towns

• Festivals	• Folk museums
• Food	• Schools of language and culture
• Music	• Ethnic holidays
• Dance	• Ethnic clubs
• Clothing	• Foreign language
• Statues	• Ethnic-affiliated institutions (banks, churches, etc.)
• Architecture	• Ethnic newspapers
• Arts and crafts	

may have developed to supply this demand. The town's residents may have come together on special holidays and brought out their revered traditions, such as food and song and dance, as ways to celebrate. They may have more frequently reinforced their ethnic heritage on a weekly basis when they gathered together in their denominational church. They may have established local athletic or social clubs that continued some of these traditions and reinforced the strong ethnic bonds within the community. All of these elements helped to build strength and identity within the community.

Travel to heritage tourism sites in the United States began to occur with some frequency in the 1920s, and it has continued with little abatement except perhaps for some drop-off during the Great Depression of the 1930s and the war years of the 1940s. With the rise in the 1920s of the automobile in America, and the concomitant rise of the tourist industry including fast food restaurants, motels, and an improved road system—at the same time that American families were coming to have more disposable income—people began to take vacations in more distant places. Soon, some of these towns became vacation destinations and provided a demand incentive for ethnic tourism.

Meanwhile, much of the job growth was moving out of these rural areas into the cities, and these towns were seeking new sources of revenue and jobs. Some began to regard heritage tourism as a solution to their problem. By no means did all towns dominated by a single nationality transform themselves into tourist destinations, but a significant minority did so. For example, Lindsborg, Kansas, proclaimed itself to be "Little Sweden, USA" and consciously built up its tourist attractions. It is these towns that consciously built upon their ethnic culture to become tourist attractions that are of primary interest to us in this chapter. We are particularly interested in looking at the mythmaking that goes on in these places, intentionally or unintentionally, as examples of inauthenticity and misinformation—and to get a sense of how commonly this kind of misinformation occurs.[4] That exercise can inform information scholars about issues and approaches taken by the tourism industry and by scholars examining the tourism and leisure world.

A CASE STUDY IN HERITAGE TOURISM: LINDSBORG, KANSAS

In the last section, we discussed heritage tourism in the abstract. Now we look at a particular case study in order to add specificity. A successful case should be emblematic of the many ethnographic studies of these towns. Since so much of the existing scholarship has focused on small communities, we sought out one typical in that respect: Lindsborg, Kansas. One tourist on YouTube said Lindborg is "in the middle of nowhere," but that visiting it became a memorable experience.[5] We chose to study Lindsborg for three reasons. First, it developed a very strong ethnic identity—in this instance Swedish—in the middle of the United States, which residents converted into an economically viable tourist destination intended to provide tourists with an example of authentic experience. Second, scholars have published extensively about this town: dissertations, monographic articles, and media comments, making it perhaps the most well studied of these towns.[6] There are also tourist comments about the town available through YouTube.[7] Third, this case presents a detailed account that buttresses the more general and abstract discussion about these cultural heritage towns made in the previous section.

It is important to note that our goal is not to summarize all the ethnographic research conducted on Lindsborg. Instead, we look at these ethnographic studies through a particular lens, accentuating what they tell us in particular about authenticity and misinformation. Perforce, our approach requires that we ignore many other aspects of this culture site, which are well covered in these various ethnographies that we use as sources.

Lindsborg is located in almost the center of Kansas, thus in the middle of the United States and also in the large American agricultural heartland. Since its permanent settlement by European and American settlers in the nineteenth century, the region became a vast area for growing wheat and corn, and for raising some cattle and other farm animals. The towns that dotted McPherson County, including Lindsborg, hosted churches (mostly Lutheran), small colleges (such as Lindsborg's Bethany College, whose athletic teams are known as the Bethany Swedes), stores, banks, grain elevators, and schools. Lindsborg was established in 1869 by a group of Swedish immigrants, and additional Swedish settlers reinforced this heritage over the next several decades. By 1900, the population of the entire county of McPherson was just over twelve thousand, growing to twenty-six thousand in 1960. In 2020, slightly more than three thousand people, just over 10 percent of the total population of the county, resided in Lindsborg.[8] For decades, Lindsborg was no different in purpose from other communities on the Great Plains that supported the local agricultural economy. Its citizens had learned to farm in ways that made sense in Kansas, discarding practices the first-generation immigrants had brought over from Sweden in those situations where these practices did not fit the environmental realities of their new homeland. The town's buildings and even how the streets were laid out were typical of many hundreds of other communities.

The first, and even second generation, of these immigrants wanted to be very American in how they worked and lived, but without totally abandoning their home life rituals, language, and identity. In short, they behaved much like immigrants from so many other countries farming throughout the Midwest.

The scholarly studies of Lindsborg have reported that a majority of residents identified with Swedish culture and traditions to varying degrees, most intensely by the first generation of "pioneers" as they were called, but ebbing and flowing in intensity by the time of the Second World War, then reviving in the late 1940s. The dominance of the agricultural economy in town waned after the war because of automation reducing the need for farm labor. This posed an existential threat to the viability of the local economy and the town itself. There was the added concern of the flight of young people from the community, seeking jobs and education in other parts of the country. Town leaders and many citizens addressed their collective concern about the local economy by agreeing to leverage their Swedish heritage to reshape their community's image and economy in support of tourism. Lindsborg is often cited as a case study of how the residents were able to successfully transform their economy, branding their town "Little Sweden, USA," while continuing to support the local agricultural economy.[9]

If one were to read the marketing materials published by the local Chamber of Commerce, newspaper articles, and other local ephemera, one would think everyone was Swedish or Swedish-American and that the transformation from a typical Kansas town into some idealized northern Europe enclave community had originated in the 1860s and 1870s. Nothing could be farther from the truth; it was a slow process of introducing, in the 1960s through 1980s, as public rituals, ones that had previously been practiced only at home; adding new facades to otherwise Midwestern non-Swedish buildings; and overlaying a patina of idealized Swedish emblems, including the *Dala* horses that are ubiquitous in downtown Lindsborg, Swedish decorations on many private homes, and Swedish flags flying in front of many storefronts.

This transformation involved multiple activities to create Little Sweden. Public rituals celebrating the original pioneers and later the Swedishness of the community that had long been in vogue for the benefits of local residents became part of the transformation aimed at tourists, most notably the *Svensk Hyllningsfest* held every other year since before the Second World War. Storefronts were remodeled to look northern European, specifically Swedish. Swedish-themed stores opened to sell ethnically themed goods to tourists, including souvenirs, locally made or imported Swedish crafts, clothing, food, Swedish flags, *Dala* horses (see figure 3.1), and Swedish meals in restaurants.[10] Beginning in the 1960s, additional public events were created and a museum/cultural center opened. The local Lutheran college (Bethany), which had strong music and art programs dating back many decades, was drafted into the effort. This multi-faceted but thematically integrated approach has succeeded over the course of the past half-century in sustaining the local economy; employment became less dependent on agriculture—although the process took time to succeed.[11] Finally, this community established two historic sites/museums to reinforce its narrative of being of Swedish and pioneer origins.

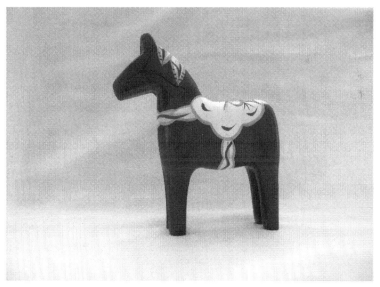

Figure 3.1 **The *Dala* horse became the iconic image of Lindsborg's campaign to brand itself as "Little Sweden."** These are carved wooden horses painted in various colors with various decorations. The original concept emerged from the province of Dalarna, Sweden, where it was a toy. *Source*: James Cortada.

Information scholars are familiar with the important cultural role of museums, archives, and libraries, so a brief glance at two of Lindsborg's museums suggest the integration of carefully crafted messages and historical realities. The McPherson County Old Mill Museum is housed in a mill built in 1897 and 1898, which operated until 1955. It was restored and transformed into a museum in 1981. On the same grounds is located a local archive/genealogical research center. Both facilities support the town's Swedish heritage. Across the street is another building, which began life as an exhibit hall at the 1904 World's Fair in St. Louis, Missouri. That building was constructed in Sweden for the purpose of the fair. After the fair, the Swedish Pavilion was purchased by an American ambassador to Sweden and shipped to Bethany College as a gift, where it served for many decades as classrooms, a small museum, and library. When it outlived its usefulness to the college, the building was moved to the location of the Old Mill Museum and partially reconstructed in 1969. Of the various Swedish-themed buildings in town, this large facility is the most important one, because it became the center hosting several Swedish-themed events each year.[12]

The site housing these several buildings—known as Heritage Square—provides the town with a space dedicated to tourists and those wishing to conduct research on the history of the community and its families. The square holds seven historic buildings, including a log cabin reputedly built in 1869. The Pavilion building's dedication ceremony in 1976, we are reminded in the current tourist literature, was attended by Swedish King Carl XVI Gustaf:[13] "The museum preserves the Swedish heritage of the Smoky Valley. The museum collects, preserves, researches, exhibits and interprets materials related to this heritage with special emphasis on the period 1870 to 1910."[14] The literature also stresses the ability to assist in Swedish genealogical research: "Do you have ancestors or relatives that once lived in Sweden? If so, our archives houses excellent resources and trained staff members to help research your Swedish ancestry. We have access to the latest online databases, including Swedish church records."[15] In short, as with many heritage communities, the museum and historical research center play a central role in Lindsborg's cultural efforts. Information scholars would find the role and messaging of these facilities familiar to them. From the perspective of the town's leaders, the fact that they established an entire campus in one location demonstrates their commitment to reinforce the community's engagement with tourists. That investment went farther than those made in many other communities, which built only a museum or an historical society or gift shop, not an entire site. The site's gift shop is only one of many retail outlets in town where one can purchase Swedish-themed items.

The journey from thinking through how to leverage tourism as an economic opportunity to its realization in the 1990s was a process than took well over three decades to navigate. These changes led to various discussions about what constituted Swedishness and authenticity, and how best to represent local history and rituals—with varying opinions among the town's residents. Comparative studies of Germanic communities in Texas, Czech communities in Nebraska, and other ethnic communities in the United States have demonstrated that the locals in Lindsborg behaved similarly to the locals in other ethnic communities. In fact, the scholarly studies of the town's historical transformation examine in detail these debates. The discussions boiled down to what image should the town exhibit (they focused primarily on idealized nineteenth-century folk traditions such as those reflected in costumes), and to what extent they had to bend to the expectations of tourists in what they thought should be a Swedish-like experience (these turned out to be festivals, costumes, food, historical exhibits, and Swedish-made or Swedish-like goods in shops).

As this process unfolded of identifying what should be portrayed that would economically benefit the town, there were heated debates about historical and cultural accuracy, and what was relevant and traditional within the town for the sake of its residents (not always or only for tourists). Older citizens complained that, by the 1980s, the town was not like in "olden times," with fewer people even knowing a smattering of the Swedish language. These older residents, as well as anthropologists, recognized that using Swedish language was a powerful culture carrier from one generation to the next, as its use buttressed ethnic rituals while reinforcing one's sense of Swedish identity. As this culture was being commercialized, many feared loss of meaning; but this was accepted collectively as a necessary risk, what one scholar studying the town's tourism called an "uneasy marriage."[16] Across the entire period, the role of authenticity and what that concept meant proved central to the town's collective discussion of their heritage and tourism. Across each facet of the town's touristic activities the meaning of authenticity as applied in this community was always present with sufficient discourse to provide fodder for three doctoral dissertations on the subject.[17] Until tourism became the main issue drawing the town's attention, locals largely ignored matters involving the authenticity of their heritage. Their costumes were whatever came to mind without specifically linking these, say, to an exact location in Sweden. Folk dancing in the 1970s led to one of the town's earliest debates about what was authentic, with some participants traveling to Sweden to lock down a precise answer. They came back realizing that there were aberrations in what they were practicing compared to the home country. In particular, they wanted their costumes to be authentic, so older costumes were no longer worn, even if they dated back many decades in the town.[18]

The town drifted toward validating its heritage by embracing concepts of nineteenth century Swedish material culture, including peasant behavior, rituals, foods, and dress. Ironically, many of the founders of the town had been poor Swedish farmers who did not want to embrace this identity; they wanted instead to become Americanized and succeed in the United States. Nevertheless, Swedish customs were introduced, such as the Christmas St. Lucia Festival, and the continuation of the town's long standing Swedish practice of the *Hyllningsfest*. Third- and fourth-generation residents introduced variations on what constituted Swedishness. They wanted to present an authentic Swedish culture, but as time passed these citizens were not as confident in the accuracy of their perspectives. Swedish nationals visiting the town commented increasingly on how the town was more "Swedish than Sweden." As one scholar noted, such concerns expressed by residents not only demonstrated how local culture was socially constructed, but also served "to codify customs that were always in a state of flux." Further, and this is a key point for scholars of information: "Selected elements of a past cultural era are latched onto as authentic, while countless other aspects of the continually evolving culture of Sweden, both historical and modern, are ignored."[19] Lindsborg was wedded to a nineteenth-century Swedish idealized peasant lifestyle. Some residents in different decades after the Second World War thought that "Swedification" of their community had gone too far—with the consequence that the local culture became less Swedish. If one views a parade video from the 2010s that supposedly celebrates the Swedish heritage, one sees marching bands playing American music, just a few people in period Swedish costumes, some antique (American-made) automobiles, and the usual assortment of local politicians and officials.[20]

Motivating participants in displaying the Swedish experience went farther than just promoting economic wellbeing. People have continually been caught up in what constituted their self-identity, and that of their families and the community at large. This was always a serious concern. All the ethnographers studying Lindsborg found that "everyone" had an opinion on these issues, but also that the majority were willing to volunteer to participate in various ways in shaping what constituted authenticity. Each festival or ritual was an occasion for airing contested views of what made particular actions more or less authentic. These debates spilled over into other topics, such as the discussions of the pseudo-Swedish facades affixed to the front of otherwise typical Kansas-styled buildings. The town council ensured that gaudy Viking-styled architecture was kept out of downtown, although eventually motels and other buildings on the outskirts incorporated some of this cartoonish architecture. Even whether to pave downtown streets with cement or asphalt, instead of continuing the use of bricks, animated people to engage in the discussion. Ultimately, the bricks were retained, despite their expense, to give the town a more "Old World" look.

One feature of authenticity that has played out in Lindsborg concerns what one ethnographer has called "consciousness." His point: "Lindsborg people have long been extraordinarily conscious of their identity and culture," and as changes to what earlier generations or differing opinions called for occurred, these acts became "symbolic" of what constituted local culture.[21] In other words, drifting away from some absolute fact of Swedishness to a new point-of-view and practice made it the new reality. Was that misinformation? The obvious answer is, "yes, of course," but only if the deviation was from a prior position that itself was factually true. The town's history suggests that the question of faithfulness to another culture was a fluid issue. It begged the question of when does a practice become factual, accurate, or authentic. Information became the messaging of marketing and branding styles, which meant some truth is shaped by currently perceived needs. Evolution of facts and manifestations of beliefs either reinforced or discouraged local citizens. In short, ambiguity ruled the day; once-and-for-all authenticity remained a continuously unfulfilled aspiration.

Ethnographers reported that evolving behavior and beliefs played out in how the town used the symbol of the red *Dala* horse. All over town there are little statues or plaques of these horses that symbolize

Sweden, although in most parts of that country it is often called by other names. In Lindsborg, these became a unifying symbol.[22] It appears on police cars, the town emblem, storefronts, decals, refrigerator magnets, and home decorations. It first appeared in the 1960s; today, one can buy miniature versions as tourist souvenirs. However, the original settlers from Sweden did not come from the part of the old country where these horses were bred. In fact, Lindsborg's immigrants came from many different regions of Sweden, so in what way was the horse emblematic of their heritage? Promoters used the horse as a convenient image, as a symbol for the entire town. Some residents saw it as a symbol of Swedishness, others of fake Swedishness and bad decision-making by the town's leaders.

The horse figures became a cultural phenomenon absent in earlier Swedish culture. Any original genuineness of the horse was effaced by commercialism, and thus remains today as both an accepted reality and a contested issue. There were related issues, such as to what extent is the *Dala* horse used to promote and commercialize heritage tourism in Lindsborg? Other cultural heritage towns such as German heritage towns in Texas face similar issues, for example, whether the Bavarian images of beer, accordion music, and *lederhosen*, which dominate image-building in towns such as Fredericksburg and Brenham, are authentic, given that the original Germanic settlers to these towns came from different cultures in the northern and central German provinces.[23] But the tourists and some locals liked the conscious implementation of this look-and-feel to their communities and their activities.

Authenticity is so fluid a concept that some ethnographers dismiss it as nearly meaningless, although practical for identifying how both local residents and tourists shape their identities. Both locals and tourists are trading in perceptions, misinformation, and reshaped interpretations of the past as they create an image of their heritage. All these perceptions in Lindsborg are contested, ambiguous, and manipulated purposefully for commercial and idealized objectives of the town's heritage. Despite the reservations of the ethnographer or information scientist, these perceptions hold a powerful reality to many citizens of Lindsborg and perhaps also to the tourists who visit there.

The scholarly discussions of Lindsborg's cultural heritage have largely ignored the mismatch between the town's cultural tourism efforts to portray an immigrant agrarian economy and its current economic and labor realities. Specifically, the economy of Lindsborg has little to do with its Swedishness today. McPherson County in the late 2010s had nearly one thousand farms, many of them large corporate enterprises. Farm income of county residents has been declining for years, and the extent that farmlands are overwhelmingly croplands, with a quarter more pastureland. The majority of crops were Midwestern, not Swedish in what was grown and how it was grown. Only 3.3 percent of Lindsborg's workforce works in agriculture, while a near equal number work in construction (3.2 percent), and a much larger 18.3 percent work in manufacturing in pharmaceutical and machine manufacturing firms. Nine percent are in retail trade—some in Swedish-centered gift shops but many in grocery and other ordinary retail establishments that one would find in any American town, such as automotive dealerships. The largest cohort of workers is employed in education (23.2 percent), in the public schools and the local college, while an additional 8.3 percent are employed in health and social services. Government employed nearly 2 percent of the total workforce.[24]

Scholars studying Lindsborg have tracked ethnic backgrounds, a normal practice when studying heritage communities. While the overwhelming majority of residents in the 1870s were of Swedish descent (indeed, born and raised in Sweden)—although increasingly from different parts of that country—the percentage declined over the course of the twentieth century. It is an important evolution, given that so many residents who support the Swedish messaging from their community link this activity to their Swedish heritage.[25] So, as the town presents itself as of Swedish descent, it simultaneously shrouds its ethnic diversity, even if accepted by the non-Swedish-heritage residents as the price for a local identity and economic opportunity. Recall that many of Lindsborg's Swedish settlers and their descendants wanted to identify more as Americans than Swedes; and, as occurred with so many other European immigrants, the third generation mostly did not speak Swedish and knew far less about their heritage.

By the 1960s, there was a question about who was of Swedish heritage, especially in the face of the "invented traditions."[26] Who was of Swedish descent was largely up to the claimant to say, although ethnographers noted that the influx of new workers and retirees in the second half of the twentieth century diluted the number of Swedish descendants. Empirical data is hard to come by. However, one analysis of a sales ledger from 1904 suggested 80 percent of the male population was then of Swedish heritage, based on last names. A 1944 telephone directory suggested that the number was now closer to 65 percent; and evidence from 1994 suggested that the percentage had dropped to 33 percent. During the US Census in 1990, 1,108 out of Lindsborg's 3,121 residents reported being of Swedish ancestry.[27] In addition to the shrinking population with a Swedish genealogical heritage was the declining knowledge of Swedish customs, rituals, beliefs, and language. These factors contributed to some resentment of the continuing Swedification of the town and attitudes about the authenticity of these efforts.

Let us conclude this chapter by abstracting some lessons about authenticity and misinformation from the Lindsborg case study:

1. In chapter 2, we discussed the differences between hot and cool authentication. Lindsborg is an example primarily of hot authentication. An environment was established, based in part on the perceived expectations of tourists about what they would find in Lindsborg that celebrated the Swedish heritage. The offerings of Lindsborg to tourists were not based on expert knowledge, for example, on scholarship of historians and archeologists. Authenticity was measured on the satisfaction level of visitors, whether they felt they had come to learn about this Swedish-American way of life (and whether they enjoyed themselves in doing so) and on that of community and business leaders.

2. Lindsborg was quite egalitarian in allowing anyone with an interest—not only trained experts—to participate in the discussions about how Lindsborg would present its Swedish heritage. The occasion for many of these discussions was the planning for how to carry out festivals for outside visitors and for the local community. The format of these events mimicked what most American towns did for purposes such as celebrating the Fourth of July.

3. There were some limited examples of cool authentication in Lindsborg. A group of citizens made a fact-finding trip to Sweden, though it does not seem to have been led by experts. The genealogical research center gave people an opportunity to learn about their own family histories through examination of the documentary record. But the genealogical center was not the fact-based driver for how Lindsborg presented itself.

4. The basic process by which Lindsborg presented its ethnic heritage was to adopt private cultural elements (food, dress,

celebrations, etc.) that were practiced in the homes of Swedish immigrants in Lindsborg, or semi-private cultural elements as practiced by the community of Swedish immigrants in the churches and social clubs of Lindsborg, transforming them into public performances.

5. This basic process was moderated by two forces, both of which were undertaken with limited factual understanding. One was the understanding of what the old country was like in the nineteenth century. The other force was understanding what visitors to Lindsborg wanted. Neither of these forces were driven by expert information gathering. For example, the information about the cultural practices in the old country conflated what went on in multiple regions of Sweden; and the decisions about what tourists wanted were not driven by careful surveying of visitors.

6. People visited Lindsborg not particularly because of the beautiful scenery or because of some signal historic event. It was mainly to experience a bit about life in a Swedish-American town. The town did not focus on showing what everyday life was like as people went about their working lives—as we will see in the next chapter was true of colonial Williamsburg in more recent times. For example, there was not an emphasis in showing visitors how a Swedish-American farm worked in the old days. Instead, the presentation of Swedish-American life was focused on festivals, dress, dance, and food.

7. As we discussed in chapter 2, place is an important issue in heritage tourism and in creating an environment that communicates authenticity. The town leaders of Lindsborg recognized this and created a central plaza near the old mill (repurposed as a museum), by moving some historic buildings and creating others all in one place where festivals could be held and tourists could focus their efforts.

8. We saw in chapter 2 (and we will explore in greater detail in chapter 4) that personal participation enhanced the visitor's experience. One way this was achieved in Lindsborg was through gift shops, where visitors could buy and take home with them a *Dala* horse or some Swedish food. It did not matter to their experience that some of these artifacts, such as the *Dala* horse, had a questionable legacy.

9. Exogenous forces drove Lindsborg to focus on being an ethnic heritage site. These forces included the spread of communication (radio, television, Internet) and transportation technologies, which made Lindsborg less isolated from the rest of America and less centered on its Swedish heritage. Another force was the rise of agricultural technologies, which changed the nature of farming and lessened work opportunities in agriculture, leading many young people to leave Lindsborg for larger cities in the region or the east or west coasts, and making the town more reliant upon tourism.

10. There is a certain irony in Lindsborg's decision to celebrate its Swedish heritage because many of the original immigrants were much more interested in assimilating and becoming more American, less so to holding on to their Swedish roots.

11. The community of Lindsborg consciously chose to focus on their Swedish heritage, even though third- and fourth-generation Swedish immigrants had less and less affiliation with Swedish culture, and despite the fact that in recent decades the majority of the population of Lindsborg had no direct Swedish roots.

In the next chapter, where we discuss Colonial Williamsburg, we explore a very different approach to how a heritage site is created and operated. But, as with Lindsborg, many of the issues faced there carry over to other locations, such as how best to shape a local identity, gain local support for the effort, and convert local initiatives in support of both economic success and as an attraction to tourists.

NOTES

1. Archived home page of Ted's Old Iron Farm and Museum is available at http://www.kansastravel.org/tedsoldironfarm.htm (accessed January 20, 2022).

2. The American Historical Association has prepared a report on the interest of the public in history, which addresses several questions of relevance here: what does the public mean by history? Why do they care about it? Where do they go for historical information? Do they find these sources trustworthy? (Peter Burkholder and Dana Schaffer, *History, the Past, and Public Culture: Results from a National Survey* [Washington, DC: American Historical Association, 2021]); see also Norman Bradburn, Robert Townsend, Carolyn Fuqua, and

John Garnett, *The Humanities in American Life: Insights from a 2019 Survey of the Public's Attitudes and Engagement* (American Academy of Arts & Sciences, 2020), https://www.amacad.org/sites/default/files/publication/downloads/The-Humanities-in-American-Life.pdf (accessed December 15, 2021); and Theresa Miller, Emilie L'Hote, and Andrew Volmert, *Communicating About History: Challenges, Opportunities, and Emerging Recommendations* (FrameWorks Institute, August 2020), https://www.frameworksinstitute.org/wp-content/uploads/2020/08/FRAJ8334-History-Strategic-Brief-200805-2-WEB.pdf (accessed December 15, 2021).

3. Statista, 2021, https://www.statista.com/statistics/241695/number-of-us-cities-towns-villages-by-population-size/.

4. There is a sizable body of literature that provides ethnographic analysis of particular American towns that trade upon their ethnic heritage. Here are a few examples: L. W. Danielson, *The Ethnic Festival and Cultural Revivalism in a Small Midwestern Town* (PhD diss. in folklore and American studies, Indiana University, 1972), https://www.proquest.com/openview/ceb3b83f3e293b8d4e81d1a2ded7e5f9/1?pq-origsite=gscholar&cbl=18750&diss=y; E. Zeitler, "Creating America's 'Czech Capital': Ethnic Identity and Heritage Tourism in Wilber, Nebraska," *Journal of Heritage Tourism* (2008); S. M. Schnell, "Creating Narratives of Place and Identity in 'Little Sweden, USA,'" *Geographical Review* (2003); H. P. Larsen, "A Windmill and a Vikinghjem: The Importance of Visual Icons as Heritage Tropes Among Danish-Americans," *Performing Nordic Heritage* (2013); J. K. Adams, "Going Deutsch: Heritage Tourism and Identity in German Texas" (PhD diss., UT Austin, 2006), https://www.proquest.com/openview/0a5d20139b9e79e43a272e1df3ed110c/1?pq-origsite=gscholar&cbl=18750&diss=y; S. M. Schnell, "The Ambiguities of Authenticity in Little Sweden, USA," *Journal of Cultural Geography* (2003); S. M. Schnell, "The Making of Little Sweden, USA," *Great Plains Quarterly* (2002); D. Chhabra, R. Healy, and E. Sils, "Staged Authenticity and Heritage Tourism," *Annals of Tourism Research* (2003), https://www.researchgate.net/profile/Deepak-Chhabra/publication/222046919_Staged_authenticity_and_heritage_tourism/links/5a25b23da6fdcc8e866b9b42/Staged-authenticity-and-heritage-tourism.pdf; Lizette Graden, "On Parade: Making Heritage in Lindsborg, Kansas," *Digitala Vetenskapliga*.

5. "Trip to Lindsborg, K," YouTube, September 7, 2017, https://www.bing.com/videos/search?q=You+Tube+Lindsborg%2c+Kansas&ru=%2fvideos%2fsearch%3fq%3dYou%2bTube%2bLindsborg%252c%2bKansas%26qpvt%3dYou%2bTube%2bLindsborg%252c%2bKansas%26FORM%3dVDRE&qpvt=You+Tube+Lindsborg%2c+Kansas&view=detail&mid=9DA61DAD451687A76C9F9DA61DAD451687A76C9F&&FORM=VDRVRV (accessed December 18, 2021).

6. Joy Kristina Adams, "Going Deutsch: Heritage Tourism and Identity in German Texas" (unpublished PhD diss., University of Texas at Austin, 2006);

Hanne Pico Larsen, "A Windmill and a *Vkinghjem*: The Importance of Visual Icons as Heritage Tropes among Danish-Americans," in *Performing Nordic Heritage: Everyday Practices and Institutional Culture*, edited by Peter Aronsson and Lizette Gradén, 73–98 (New York: Routledge, 2013); Ezra Zeitler, "Creating America's 'Czech Capital': Ethnic Identity and Heritage Tourism in Wilber, Nebraska," *Journal of Heritage Tourism* 4, no. 1 (2009): 73–85; and Steven Hoelscher, *Heritage on Stage: The Invention of Ethnic Place in America's Little Switzerland* (Madison: University of Wisconsin Press, 1998).

7. See, for example on YouTube, "Lindsborg Kansas—Little Sweden," (October 3, 2017); "Little Sweden USA—Lindsborg, Kansas" (September 30, 2016); "Svensk Hyliningsfest 2019" (October 22, 2019), "Lindsborg, Kansas: Perfect for Families" (July 13, 2017) (all accessed December 20, 2021).

8. US Census Bureau.

9. For example, Lizette Gradén, "On Parade," Schnell, "Little Sweden, USA."

10. The strategy is well summarized by Steven M. Schnell, "The Ambiguities of Authenticity in Little Sweden," *Journal of Cultural Geography* 20, no. 2 (2003): 43–68, based on his dissertation research conducted in the 1990s.

11. In 2020, unemployment in the town hovered at 2.4 percent. Later we discuss the diversity of employment which demonstrates that not all workers were engaged in Swedish-centered activities, US Census Bureau.

12. Elisabeth Thorsell, "The Old Mill Museum of Lindsborg, Kansas," *Swedish American Genealogist* 28, no. 1 (2008): article 9, https://digitalcommons.augustana.edu/cgi/viewcontent.cgi?article=1754&context=swensonsag (accessed December 9, 2021).

13. McPherson County, KS, "1904 World's Fair Swedish Pavilion," https://www.mcphersoncountyks.us/377/1904-Worlds-Fair-Swedish-Pavilion (accessed December 9, 2021).

14. Old Mill Museum, home page https://www.oldmillmuseum.org/ (accessed December 9, 2021).

15. Old Mill Museum, "Swedish Research," https://www.oldmillmuseum.org/swedish-research/ (accessed December 9, 2021).

16. Schnell "The Ambiguities of Authenticity in Little Sweden, USA," 49.

17. Wayne Wheeler, *An Analysis of Social Change in a Swedish-American Community: The Case of Lindsborg, Kansas* (New York: AMS Press, 1986); Gradén, *On Parade*; Schnell, "Little Sweden, USA."

18. Schnell, "The Ambiguities of Authenticity in Little Sweden, USA," 188–200.

19. Schnell, "The Ambiguities of Authenticity in Little Sweden, USA," 52. Examples of what were left out included Swedish beliefs in witchcraft in earlier times and contemporary national political and social policies after the First and Second World Wars, which were contrary to the conservative political beliefs

of many in central Kansas, Schnell, "The Ambiguities of Authenticity in Little Sweden, USA," 52–54.

20. "2019 Hyllningsfest Parade—Lindsborg, KS," YouTube, October 20, 2019, https://www.youtube.com/watch?v=fHy1VZGPKmc (accessed December 6, 2021).

21. Schnell, "Creating Narratives of Place and Identity in 'Little Sweden, USA,'" 57.

22. Lena Johannesson, "On Folk Art and Other Modernities," in *Swedish Folk Art: All Tradition is Change*, edited by B. Klein and M. Widbom, 44 (New York: Harry N. Abrams, 1994); Schnell, "Creating Narratives of Place and Identity in '"Little Sweden, USA,'" 315–25; and for the same kind of analysis of the role of material culture as symbols, see Lizette Gradén, "Christmas in Lindsborg," in *Creating Diversities: Folklore, Religion and the Politics of Heritage*, edited by Anna-Leena Siikala, Barbro Klein, and Stein R. Mathisen, 276–91 (Helsinki: Finnish Literature Society, 2004), which focuses on the role of porcelain miniatures of Swedish buildings in the town.

23. Joy Kristina Adams, "Going *Deutsch*: Heritage Tourism and Identity in German Texas" (unpublished PhD diss, University of Texas at Austin, 2006): 60–184, 238–42.

24. All statistics drawn from US Census Bureau, US Department of Agriculture, and McPherson County. The latter does not emphasize heritage tourism, rather employment in energy, equipment manufacturing, life sciences and higher education, https://www.mcphersoncountyks.us/ (accessed December 8, 2021).

25. US Census Bureau. One might add, as of 2019, slightly less than 90 percent of Lindsborg residents are White non-Hispanic and 5 percent are White Hispanics. Three percent are African American. Everyone in the town uses English as their primary language.

26. Schnell, "Creating Narratives of Place and Identity in '"Little Sweden, USA,'" 236.

27. Schnell, "Creating Narratives of Place and Identity in '"Little Sweden, USA,'" 334.

4

AUTHENTICITY IN LARGE PRIVATE HERITAGE TOURISM SITES

THE CASE OF COLONIAL WILLIAMSBURG

[Referring to Colonial Williamsburg:] As phony as a nine-dollar bill.[1]

Departure from truth here and there will inevitably produce a cumulative deterioration of authenticity and consequent loss of public confidence.[2]

[T]he idea of authenticity has changed over time. Authenticity is neither a static concept nor a fact. Individuals, cultures, and societies categorize things as authentic versus inauthentic, and these categories are built on tangible and intangible aspects of objects, such as their designs or history of use.[3]

This chapter examines authenticity in large private heritage tourism sites, primarily through a case study of Colonial Williamsburg, which is the largest open air tourism site in the United States. These large museums have annual operating budgets ranging in size from a quarter million dollars to tens of millions of dollars. The annual visitor counts at these sites range from a few thousand to more than a million. These sites often have paid employees, ranging from several to hundreds. They tend to have at least one paid curatorial staff member, though a few of the largest have several hundred. Among these curatorial members there are typically at least a few who have formal education, often a doctorate in a relevant discipline such as history or anthropology. However, much of the work of presenting the artifacts to the public, and even in cataloguing and conserving these artifacts belongs to young college graduates with more interest than education, or to those older volunteers who are keenly interested but not necessarily professionally educated. Some but by no means all these heritage sites have established programs to train their less experienced employees and volunteers; and many of these people take it upon themselves to educate themselves on the relevant topics.

These heritage sites tend to be more financially stable than the small heritage sites, through a combination of donations from individuals and corporations, ticket revenue, and sales revenue from their gift shops. On average, these museums tend to be less likely to proffer misinformation than the small museums, but there is a wide variation in practices. These museums raise a new set of questions about what authenticity is in a heritage site.

We focus here on Colonial Williamsburg. It is an example of a living history site that tries to re-create a time and place in American history—in this case eighteenth-century Colonial Virginia. There are a number of other examples of large, private historical re-creation heritage sites, for example, the Henry Ford Museum and Greenfield Village in Michigan, Sturbridge Village in Massachusetts, Mystic Seaport Museum in Connecticut, and Old Cowtown Museum in Kansas. Of course, there are other kinds of large, private heritage sites in the United States that are not devoted to recreation of a particular historic environment. Some of the larger and best known include the historic houses Winterthur in Delaware and Monticello in Virginia,[4] the art museum and gardens of the Barnes Foundation in Philadelphia, the Carnegie Museum of Natural History in Pittsburgh, and the Huntington Library, Art Museum, and Botanical Gardens in California.

Because of its size and quality, its historical importance, and its identification with precepts of freedom and the American Revolution, Colonial Williamsburg has been extensively studied by a variety of different academic disciplines, including architects and art historians interested in aesthetic archetypes, historians interested in historiography, anthropologists interested in the epistemology of the authentic, and philosophers interested in phenomenology. The plan here is to summarize their findings about Colonial Williamsburg in a way that is useful to information scholars and the general reader, especially on the issue of authenticity.

Williamsburg is a town with a population, in 2020, of approximately fifteen thousand, located in the Tidewater region of Virginia between the James and York rivers, both of which channel into the southern end of the Chesapeake Bay. Williamsburg is located approximately fifty miles east-southeast of Richmond, the current state capitol of Virginia. The town was founded in the early 1630s and itself served as the state capitol from 1699 to 1780.[5] As such, it was an important site in American colonial history—a place closely affiliated with the forming of the new American Republic. A few of the many famous names associated Williamsburg in the eighteenth century include George Washington, Thomas Jefferson, James Madison, James Monroe, John Tyler, and George Mason. It is the home of the College of William & Mary, the second oldest university in the United States (founded in 1693) and today a vital public research university.[6] The main segment of Colonial Williamsburg, the historical re-creation heritage site, stands in an approximately half-mile by one-mile rectangular parcel of land, centrally located within the town and adjacent to the college.

ABOUT COLONIAL WILLIAMSBURG

The story of the founding of Colonial Williamsburg is well known, so we will only summarize here.[7] W. A. R. Goodwin, the rector of Bruton Parish Church in Williamsburg and later a religious studies professor at William & Mary, already had been advocating for historical preservation for more than twenty years. In the mid-1920s, he began to approach various wealthy Americans, including Henry Ford, about the reconstruction of the original village of Williamsburg as it had existed in the eighteenth century.[8] In 1926 he captured the interest of John D. Rockefeller Jr.,[9] who, with his wife Abby Aldrich Rockefeller, provided the initial and largest funding of Colonial Williamsburg—with their total donations over time amounting to $68 million.[10] Later, other wealthy individuals including Lila and DeWitt Wallace and Walter Annenberg also provided major donations. Other support came through donations from the general public (some fifty thousand donors), ticket sales, and revenue from the shops, taverns, inns, and golf course run by the Colonial Williamsburg Foundation. By the mid-1930s, the historical site was seeing more than one hundred thousand visitors per year; by the 1980s, the number was more than one million per year.

More than four hundred new buildings were built and eighty-eight structures (both residences and commercial) were restored to the colonial style of the eighteenth century. Many post-eighteenth-century buildings on the site were purchased from private homeowners and business owners and destroyed. The Colonial Williamsburg Foundation also acquired land adjacent to the historic site to provide pastoral views from the town, much as a person living there would have had in the eighteenth century. The Foundation also arranged for the state highway that went through the site to be re-routed, and they rebuilt the nearby railroad station in a colonial style. Numerous homes and businesses on the site were opened to visitors, some showing trade people carrying out their crafts as they would have done them in the eighteenth century. Costumed interpreters roam the grounds, interacting with the visitors. Extensive gardens were added, and efforts were made to preserve and re-introduce livestock that would have been common in the eighteenth century.[11] Over time, a major archival, conservation, and research library and two art museums were added, as was a major program to offer training to public school teachers. Also constructed on the site are various places where visitors can eat, lodge, or buy gifts.

The research program at Colonial Williamsburg does not focus narrowly on the history of Williamsburg itself. There is an active program of research on Colonial and Revolutionary history and on American decorative and folk arts. The art museums have continuously been acquiring artifacts and today hold more than sixty thousand items in the fine and decorative arts.[12] Extensive library and archival holdings support these efforts.

TOWN-FOUNDATION RELATIONS IN THE BUILDING AND ONGOING OPERATIONS OF COLONIAL WILLIAMSBURG

We saw in our case study of Lindsborg that the heritage activities provided some much-needed economic development to the town but that it was not pervasive in the everyday lives of the residents. Many went on with their daily lives in farming or at the college, aware of the Swedish heritage activities but only occasionally affected by them, such as on the days on which the town held a festival and the town was swollen with outsiders. The story was different in Williamsburg, where a sizable piece of the center of town was taken up by the living history museum, numerous people were displaced from their homes and 790 houses destroyed, the major highway through town was rerouted, many of the downtown businesses were replaced by new ones associated with the heritage site, and in some years as many as three thousand tourists visited (on average) each day of the year. In this section, we explore how this major disruption sat with the residents of the town. We focus on the initial building of Colonial Williamsburg, in the period from the late 1920s until the beginning of the Second World War in the early 1940s.

Land and buildings were bought for Colonial Williamsburg anonymously as much as possible, to hide the name of John D. Rockefeller Jr. under the belief that sale prices would rise if his name became known. There were numerous planning meetings with the town's residents and significant contact between the representatives of the Foundation and the homeowners. For the most part, the town was supportive of the creation of Colonial Williamsburg, although there were occasional concerns as expressed by Major S. D. Freeman, a retired army officer who was serving as the president of the local school board:

> No consideration has been given to the broader aspects of this transfer. If you give up your land, it will no longer be *your* city. Will you feel the same pride in it that you now feel as you walk across the Greens, or down the broad streets? Have you all been hypnotized by five million dollars dangled before your eyes? Can anyone of you talk back to five million dollars? If we close the contract, what will happen when the matter passes out of the hands of Dr. Goodwin and Mr. Rockefeller, in both of whom we have perfect confidence?... Who will control?... We will reap dollars, but will we own our town? Will you not be in the position of a butterfly pinned to a card in a glass cabinet, or like a mummy unearthed in the tomb of Tutankhamen.[13]

Williamsburg had been a sleepy town, not a hub of strong economic activity; and the heritage site was seen as a way to attract economic development to the area. In particular, much of the reconstruction took place during the height of the Great Depression, and Colonial Williamsburg provided many good jobs at a time when unemployment was high elsewhere in the United States.[14] Also, there was strong local support for the beautification of Williamsburg that came with the high quality of architectural restoration and the creation of beautiful gardens and landscapes by the Foundation.[15]

There were three significant local objections to the building of Colonial Williamsburg. The most serious involved the African American community, which did not participate in the planning process. Williamsburg's population contained slightly more Blacks than Whites at the time the restoration began, and the part of town being razed for the heritage site was a relatively integrated neighborhood of Blacks and Whites. The African American community was unhappy that they tended to receive less compensation for their homes than White residents did, three Black churches were razed in the course of the restoration process and only one was rebuilt (only after the church sued and the Foundation agreed to build a new church away from the heritage site). Also, the displacement led to higher Black-White segregation in town, when most of the Blacks were moved to three less central and less desirable locations that ended up being all Black. Through a combination of Black flight and White population growth, by the end of the 1930s, only 23 percent of the population in Williamsburg was Black.[16]

The second objection concerned local businesses. A number of the local businesses were located near Duke of Gloucester Street, and all of these had to be moved for the restoration. The Foundation created a commercial site (Merchants Square) just west of Colonial Williamsburg, and a number of these businesses located there. However, rising rents and the competition for space from tourist-oriented businesses eventually drove out the local businesses.

The third objection concerned a Civil War monument, which had been erected in the Palace Green in 1908, that was moved from the center of town for the restoration, to the outskirts of town and placed in a local cemetery. Although Colonial Williamsburg was intended to be a national attraction, Williamsburg was still a Southern town; and the relocation did not sit well with many of the White residents who had family members who had fought in the war. A group sued, and the monument was relocated to stand in front of the new courthouse. There it stood until 2020, when the city council voted to remove it and present it to the private United Daughters of the Confederacy.[17]

GOODWIN'S VISION FOR COLONIAL WILLIAMSBURG, AND THE PROBLEMS OF EQUATING AUTHENTICITY WITH HISTORICAL EXACTITUDE

There are two important guiding principles in Goodwin's work on Colonial Williamsburg that help us to understand the notion of authenticity in the early years of the historic site—from the founding in the 1920s until the end of the 1950s. The first principal concerns the purpose of Colonial Williamsburg. Some scholars have noted that Goodwin was a religious man and that he appropriated religious language in describing the purpose of Colonial Williamsburg.[18] As one of these scholars described Goodwin's purpose, "[The historic site] would not be a temple to God, but a temple to America and its foundational ideals of liberty, freedom, and patriotism. Goodwin hoped to offer Americans a secular religion dedicated to the values of the past."[19] As Goodwin himself stated, Colonial Williamsburg would be "a shrine that would bear witness to the faith and the devotion and the sacrifice of the nation builders."[20] This meant building a historical site that was meant to honor the patriotic acts of the founding fathers in their selfless efforts to create liberty and freedom for the American people. Goodwin hoped that this homage would deliver an educational and inspirational message to Americans of his time (and, indeed, to others around the world); or as Goodwin expressed it: "by making America more conscious of its heritage, will help to develop a more highly educated and consequently a more devoted spirit of patriotism."[21] This meant that in its first few decades, Colonial Williamsburg focused on the lives of these mostly White, male, educated leaders and less on the other members of the eighteenth-century Williamsburg community.

The second guiding principle was to value authenticity and to define it in terms of historical exactitude. As Goodwin stated (in an extension of an epigraph that begins this chapter):

> If there is one firm guiding and restraining word which should be passed on to those who will be responsible for the restoration in the future, that one word is integrity. A departure from truth here and there will inevitably produce a cumulative deterioration of authenticity and consequent loss of public confidence.[22]

Architecture, household and business furnishings, gardens and open space, clothing, food, work crafts, and other aspects of the historical site (for example, publications and the statements of the costumed tour guides) should be made as historically accurate for eighteenth-century Williamsburg as possible. While original furniture from this period might not exist, painstaking research should be undertaken to make what appeared on the historic site faithful to what appeared in the town in the eighteenth century.

Unfortunately, this guiding principle had two shortcomings—one logical and one psychological. The statement "all aspects of Colonial Williamsburg must have historical exactitude" is a universal statement, and it is a well understood principle of logic that a single instance of something from Colonial Williamsburg that was not accurate would make this universal claim false. Moreover, a single instance of inaccuracy has the psychological effect of casting doubt among the visitors to the historic site, as the following quotation nicely explains:

> The clothing is just as important as creating an accurate interior, creating any sort of accuracy. Any time you have a break in your credibility, then everything that is credible is lost, or it's called into question. If you have someone who comes in, and they happen to see plastic buttons, or someone wearing obvious knee socks, instead of proper hosiery, then to me that's saying, well, that's not accurate. I wonder if the way that tea service is laid out is accurate? I wonder if the fact that that garden's laid out the way it is, I wonder if that's accurate? You start to lose it. That's why it's so important that our interpreters have the ability to take things that are less than accurate and get people to start thinking beyond them. And catching people, anticipating problems of credibility. Now if we can catch them up, by using better tools, better floor arrangements, better costumes, better gardens, then that's one less chink in our credibility armor that we have to worry about.[23]

One of the approaches to building this credibility armor was to conduct unprecedented amounts of research as the buildings were being renovated or reconstructed. Great effort and funding was devoted to this goal. In 1926, the foundation hired a top architectural firm (Perry, Shaw, and Hepburn) and established an advisory board of leading architects, which operated from 1928 to 1948, to advise on the historically faithful reconstruction of buildings.

> [The architectural firm] made a detailed study of Williamsburg and also sent searchers to every important library in America for information. The William and Mary College Library, the State Library and the Clement Library at Ann Arbor were all ransacked. The Historical Society and State Conservation and Development Commission unearthed unexpected

"finds." The Huntingdon Library in California produced original drawings by Jefferson giving the plan of the main building of the College itself with proposed additions. Parties were sent to England, France, Spain and Italy. They searched London's Record Office and the British Museum, the State Library of France, the Great Library in Seville and the world-famous Vatican Library. Dr. Goodwin and the architects visited all the great Colonial houses remaining in the northern Tidewater area, the homes of the former Virginian aristocracy—historic places such as Shirley, Berkeley and Westover. They left no stone unturned in their efforts to find authentic evidence.[24]

A wide range of documentary sources were used in the effort to attain historical accuracy, for example, "advertisements, merchants' accounts, personal letters, wills, estate inventories, and probate records."[25] The archeology program of Colonial Williamsburg today holds half a million artifacts. There were detailed household inventories for furnishings of households and that made accurate furnishing possible.[26] But in other cases, such as the gardens of Williamsburg, the task proved more difficult:

> less information rewarded the searchers as practically every foot of this historic ground had been fought over several times, and few written documents were discovered. Consequently, over 100 historic Virginian gardens were studied: widths and lengths of garden paths, relation of outbuildings to main houses, vegetation, etc., etc. English gardens of the same period came under scrutiny and disclosed that the form of the colonial garden was generally about a quarter of a century behind those in England. Plant lists of the time, old family letters, and records of Arnold Arboretum, all made it clear that some of the most successful English plants would not thrive for long in the hot summer months of Virginia.[27]

Indeed, Colonial Williamsburg is regarded as a leading center in these areas of research.[28]

Archeological evidence and records from the eighteenth century were consulted to reconstruct buildings when the major reconstruction efforts were carried out in the 1930s.[29] Over time, the staff—mostly historians, archeologists, and curators—responsible for producing this historical accuracy grew and grew. By 1989, the Foundation employed 160 historians, curators, and conservators. Contrast that staffing with the United Kingdom's Historic Trust, mentioned at the beginning of chapter 1, which maintains numerous historic sites across the Kingdom but only employs three curators and conducts no research or archeological projects.[30]

No matter how much research the staff and outside consultants do, there are bound to be historical inaccuracies. The historical site contains thousands of artifacts and there are numerous historical topics that might interest visitors. The historical documentation is imperfect, and the staff cannot possibly have studied up on every topic that might conceivably be of interest to visitors. And humans simply make mistakes from time to time. Anthropologists Eric Gable and Richard Handler have astutely identified three means by which the staff defuse criticisms from visitors and defend Colonial Williamsburg's claim to authenticity: by pointing out that Colonial Williamsburg has made mistakes in the past but has taken steps to correct them; by pointing out that Colonial Williamsburg is simultaneously used as an eighteenth-century recreation and a contemporary town (e.g., noting that some of the staff live in some of the historic buildings and they have all the everyday needs of modern living that the visitors do in their own homes); and by noting that some inaccuracies come from making the historic area more suitable for visitors (e.g., by lining Duke of Gloucester Street with shade trees, even though they would not have existed in the eighteenth century, in order to make the town more comfortable for visitors during the hot, humid Virginia summers).[31]

"SILK PANTS PATRIOTS" AND "THE FINER THINGS": HOW ROCKEFELLER'S ELITE AESTHETIC VISION CHALLENGED AUTHENTICITY

Abby Rockefeller died in 1948, and her husband (John D. Rockefeller Jr.) was less actively involved with Colonial Williamsburg after her death. (He died in 1960.) During the period of their active involvement with this heritage site, they strongly supported the two hallmarks of Goodwin's vision for Colonial Williamsburg: the celebration of a golden, Revolutionary era that embodied the American ideals of freedom, liberty, and patriotism; and the focus on authenticity as defined by extreme historical accuracy.[32] However, there was a third hallmark in the Rockefellers support of Colonial Williamsburg: an elite aesthetic, which involved an appreciation of the finer things in life, such as beautiful buildings with beautiful furnishings, embedded in a harmonious natural landscape, where culture could thrive. As Rockefeller himself stated the purpose: "the restoration of Williamsburg... offered an opportunity to restore a complete area and free it entirely from alien and inharmonious surroundings, as well as to preserve the beauty and charm of the old buildings and gardens of the city and its historic significance."[33] This idyll of eighteenth-century life was to be contrasted to modern society of the 1930s that faced the ravages of industrialization, urbanization with its attendant disease and poverty, the economic upheaval of the Great Depression, the rise of fascism in Europe, and the threat of world war.

This third hallmark was entirely consonant with the first of Goodwin's hallmarks, for most of the people celebrated in Colonial Williamsburg were these wealthy White individuals, such as Washington and Jefferson, who were leaders in the patriotic movement—who the curators at the historic site sometimes sneeringly called the "silk pants patriots."[34] As Rockefeller himself wrote: "[Colonial Williamsburg] teaches of the patriotism, high purpose, and unselfish devotion of our forefathers for the common good."[35] The third hallmark was, however, only selectively consonant with the second hallmark. On the one hand, the Rockefellers insisted on Colonial Williamsburg being recreated at a high standard of excellence, and their deep pockets was what made possible the costly extensive research and fine craftsmanship that enabled Goodwin to pursue his goal of historical accuracy. On the other hand, their sense of elite aestheticism meant that attention was only applied to these wealthy historical figures and not to the much larger population of ordinary farmers, tradesmen and workmen, women, the mentally incapacitated, and the incarcerated; moreover, sometimes the Rockefellers pursued their elite aesthetic in ways that did not conform with historical accuracy, for example, in how they furnished their own home in Colonial Williamsburg.[36]

As a number of scholars have noted, the particular buildings that the Rockefellers paid to have renovated or rebuilt in the early years of Colonial Williamsburg is telling. Their earliest reconstructions included the Capitol Building and the Governor's Palace, seats of power in eighteenth-century Williamsburg; the Raleigh Tavern, where the wealthy members of eighteenth-century Williamsburg congregated; and what was renamed the Wren Building on the William & Mary campus, which had luster because of its affiliation with the world-renowned British architect Christopher Wren (See figure 4.1).[37] In rebuilding the Capitol, the Foundation chose to reconstruct the one from 1705, which burned

Figure 4.1 This image is of the restored Governor's Palace in Williamsburg, Virginia. Construction of the original building began in 1706 and was reconstructed in 1931. It had been destroyed in 1781 due to a fire. This image illustrates Colonial Williamsburg's effort to place visitors in an environment that mimics that of the 1700s. Here the rider is dressed in period clothing, while the horse's tack, is also meticulously replicated to reflect eighteenth century styles. *Source:* Library of Congress, LC-DIG-highsm-61326.

down, rather than the one that stood in 1770 because the earlier one had a grander architectural design; and the architects knowingly deviated from the way the building had looked in 1705, giving it a symmetry that it did not originally possess because they thought their design better represented an architectural ideal.

Rockefeller was also concerned about the outside details of Colonial Williamsburg. He insisted that the buildings and fences be repainted every year, the gardens be recreated in an eighteenth-century style, and the town be kept clean, for example with the main road paved and prompt removal of horse droppings. There were few signs of poverty in the recreated town, even though that had been a part of eighteenth-century life. Rockefeller lived in Colonial Williamsburg part of the time, and he wanted it to be a place he felt comfortable coming home to. However, this high level of maintenance and cleanliness was not authentic to eighteenth-century Williamsburg. For example, it is said of Duke of Gloucester Street, the main avenue in town, that it is a mile long, one hundred feet wide, and two feet deep—the latter dimension referring to the amount of mud present during the rainy season.[38] It was also noted that the reproduction furniture displayed at Colonial Williamsburg during the Rockefeller era was of higher quality than would have been found in eighteenth-century Williamsburg.

The story of the Abby Aldrich Rockefeller Folk Art Museum, the first museum in the United States dedicated to American folk art, also demonstrates this elite aesthetic hallmark. The museum, which holds folk art from the 1720s to the present—not just the eighteenth century—is located on the edge of the historic district of Colonial Williamsburg and operated by the Foundation. Abby Rockefeller was one of the founders of the Museum of Modern Art in New York City in 1929, and she and her husband were major donors to the museum over the years. Holger Cahill, an art dealer in New York, convinced Abby that folk art was an important indigenous art form and connected in meaningful ways to the modern art movement. Abby began collecting folk art avidly in the early 1930s.

The Rockefellers purchased Bassett Hall, the grandest private residence in the historic district of Colonial Williamsburg, renovated it, and lived in it part time. Abby decorated the house not with colonial antiquities or reproductions, but instead with items from her folk art collection.[39] The bulk of her collection was shown publicly in another house in the historic district, the Ludwell-Paradise House. Upon Abby's death, a new museum was created in her honor, with her collection and that of her son David forming the bulk of the original collection, and with an endowment provided by her husband. One of the rationales for moving the collection to a new building—aside from the need for extra space and better facilities for exhibition—was that many pieces in the folk art collection did not fit the authenticity criteria for the historic district of displaying only things used or made in eighteenth-century Williamsburg.[40]

The story of the other art museum at Colonial Williamsburg, the DeWitt Wallace Decorative Arts Museum, also represents the elite aesthetic theme, but at a later time. The museum came about through a large donation of DeWitt Wallace and his wife Lila Bell Acheson Wallace, who had created *Reader's Digest* in 1922 and made a fortune from its publication. The donation enabled Colonial Williamsburg to both open the museum adjacent to the historic site and renovate the nearby mental hospital, on the historic site, dating from 1773. The museum holds a wide collection of British and American decorative arts covering the years 1670 to 1840—so, thus again beyond the purview of Colonial Williamsburg. The opening paragraph on the museum's website refers to the elite aesthetic motif, where it says, "The DeWitt Wallace Decorative Arts Museum houses a variety of the 'finer things.'"[41] The Wallace Museum also has a Rockefeller connection. Abby's son Laurence was a friend of DeWitt Wallace and a member of the board of directors of *Reader's Digest*, and it was he who encouraged the Wallaces to become major donors to the Colonial Williamsburg Foundation.[42]

In the late 1920s and throughout the 1930s, Colonial Williamsburg was marketed primarily to a better educated and more wealthy population.[43] After all, during the Great Depression it was a wealthier clientele who had the luxury of time free from work and the funds to travel. Both beauty and lifestyle, as well as the historical importance of the site, was presented by the public relations office. For example, one article in *Better Homes and Gardens* was titled "Williamsburg, The Ideal Home Town" and noted that the town was attractive to people who wanted to "step back two centuries... to gracious living."[44] These messages were consonant with the refined living message of the Rockefellers.

Because so much of the early development at Williamsburg had involved the restoration of buildings, it is not surprising that *Architectural Digest*, a publication with a high-end readership, had regular feature articles about the historic site.[45] These articles supported Goodwin's argument that authenticity was achieved through historical accuracy, focusing, for example, on the extensive detective work taken to learn how to accurately recapture eighteenth-century architectural details in the renovations and reconstructions. Other publications with feature articles about Colonial Williamsburg during this time included magazines about travel (*Automobilist, American Motorist, C&O* [the magazine of the C&O railroad]), architecture (*Architectural Record*), and homes and gardens (*Good Housekeeping, House Beautiful, Better Homes & Gardens*)—all of which appealed to middle- and upper-class readerships.

From the 1960s onward, Colonial Williamsburg was fundamentally changed by social history, as we describe below, to achieve a new version of authenticity that involved the lives of everyday folks, not just the silk pants patriots. But even in these more recent times, there were certain people who persisted in their appreciation of the elite aesthetic, the beautiful living that characterized Colonial Williamsburg in the Rockefeller years. Gable and Handler tell a story of an older woman returning to the historic site, staying at the Williamsburg Inn located on the historic site, and remembering how life had been in the early years:[46]

> She had been eating in the luxurious dining room and, desiring sugar for her coffee, was about to dip her spoon into a large pewter cup in front of her when a liveried black waiter quickly bent over, moved the cup, and spooned sugar from a smaller container into her coffee. The first container, she elaborated, was salt. Apparently, in colonial times, she added, they served salt in what today might look like a sugar bowl. But it wasn't the inn's attention to that little piece of authenticity that she wanted us to see through her eyes. Rather, it was the black waiter's silent skill. Ever attentive, waiting unobtrusively but alertly in the background, he'd anticipated her faux pas and resolved her problem without calling attention to her mistake. Skilled waiters like that, she emphasized, could not be reproduced, or faked, or trained. They embodied for her the essence of what Colonial Williamsburg used to stand for before "that new word, 'authenticity,' "had become such a concern.

CRITICISMS OF AUTHENTICITY IN COLONIAL WILLIAMSBURG

In this section, we briefly identify six criticisms of Colonial Williamsburg, mostly from scholars but also from tourists visiting the site. All of them, in one way or another are related to inauthenticity. Each of them is separate from the others, but there are connections between some of these criticisms, for example, between 3 and 4, or between 5 and 6. For the most part, there were few criticisms prior to or during the Second World War. In fact, most of these criticisms began to show up in the 1970s and 1980s, in part because of the influence of the new social history and the application of constructivist thought to Colonial Williamsburg.

1. *Compromises due to the presence of contemporary use of the historic site.* These criticisms might include the shade trees that were not present in the eighteenth century but were useful for protecting visitors from the summer heat; or the existence of trash cans, modern kitchens, and modern bathrooms in historic houses that were being used as residences for staff members. These compromises seemed acceptable to the public because they understood that the Colonial Williamsburg staff recognized them as historically incorrect but tolerated them for some other purpose. There was an effort to ameliorate this issue, for example, by hiding the trash cans behind hedges, so that the public would not so readily see them.

2. *Historical inadequacies.* These were items that the Colonial Williamsburg staff intended to make historically accurate but failed to do so. One example concerned the food that was served in the taverns on site and appeared in the cookbooks published by the Foundation. Food historians have taken great umbrage to a recipe that calls for corn syrup, an ingredient not known until well into the nineteenth century that appeared in *Recipes from America's Restored Villages*,[47] or the unlikelihood that the recipe for Captain Rasmussen's Clam Chowder would have included garlic, green peppers, tomatoes, and tomato puree in the eighteenth century as is claimed in *Famous Meals from Williamsburg.*[48] We imagine that visitors to the Williamsburg tavern may have been more tolerant of these inaccuracies because original ingredients were not so easy to come by and the ingredients available to eighteenth-century cooks might not have been found so palatable by late twentieth-century diners.[49] Perhaps tourists visiting Colonial Williamsburg would be less accepting of an interpreter wearing nail polish, plastic earrings, and tennis shoes, something that was easier to spot as

inauthentic and also something easy to avoid. In fact, when an elderly couple complained about this behavior, the president of Colonial Williamsburg was quick to let the visitors know that these behaviors were going to be quickly rectified.[50]

3. *Focus on the elite members of the Williamsburg community rather than on the entire population.* The historical presentation of the elite population was mostly accurate, and it was well received by visitors to Colonial Williamsburg who were looking for hero worship or patriotic inspiration. However, this focus was anathema to the new social historians, who wanted to present the stories of everyday life of all the residents in eighteenth-century Williamsburg. Indeed, most of the criticism of this sort came from scholars and other cultural critics after the new social history had become widely spread and accepted.

4. *Tensions between history as facts and history as interpretation.* For some visitors, and for the early founders of Colonial Williamsburg, there was a sense that there is a single master narrative and the historic site should be telling it. For people with that perspective, it was simply a matter of providing correctness in the visual images of the buildings, realistic furnishings, and accurate factual data in the stories from interpreters and the Foundation's publications. Closely associated with the adoption of the new social history was an attitude that history is not about facts but instead about interpretation, and that these interpretations are constructed by humans, who have reasons (whether conscious or not) for what they choose to present or not present and how they spin the meaning of various incidents and artifacts. As Gable and Handler explain this point: "the new historians at Colonial Williamsburg were explicitly constructivists. Not only did they wish to replace a patriotic history with one that was more critical, they wanted to teach the public that history making itself was not simply a matter of facts and truth. It was, instead, a process shot through with hidden cultural assumptions and ideological agendas."[51]

5. *Leaving too little to the imagination.* As Gable and Handler argue in a different article, "for other people, Colonial Williamsburg is the last place they'd choose to visit, let alone live. 'The place leaves nothing to the imagination,' a colleague of ours who prefers ruins keeps pointing out. In this critical perspective, a ruin invites visi-

tors to populate and rebuild the past in their own minds, whereas a restoration like Colonial Williamsburg renders them passive spectators with no role other than the consumption of kitsch."[52] This criticism is similar to the one offered by the reader of the novel, who wants to create their own version of the world and who is critical of the film made from that novel. For these people, the authentic world of the novel is the one created in their mind, not one created by a Hollywood writer and director.

6. *Favoring entertainment over education.* Goodwin and Rockefeller were keen to make Colonial Williamsburg an educational experience, teaching visitors about the founding fathers and what they had to say about patriotism in modern times. It has become commonplace, however, to hear Colonial Williamsburg described as a version of Disneyland, a place of fantasy rather than truth. The most vocal articulation of this position was by the architecture critic Ada Louise Huxtable, who wrote in her 1997 book, *The Unreal America: Architecture and Illusion*:

> The replacement of reality with selective fantasy is a phenomenon of that most successful and staggeringly profitable American phenomenon, the reinvention of the environment as themed entertainment. The definition of "place" as a chosen image probably started in a serious way in the late 1920s at Colonial Williamsburg, predating and paving the way for the new world order of Walt Disney Enterprises. Certainly it was in the restoration of Colonial Williamsburg that the studious fudging of facts received its scholarly imprimatur, and that history and place as themed artifact hit the big time.[53]

As we can see, the time at which these criticisms held the most sway differed from criticism to criticism; and whether it was the scholar, cultural critic, staff member, or visiting tourist who made them also varied. All, however, are at least implicitly indictments against authenticity.

WHOSE HISTORY? THE NEW SOCIAL HISTORY AND THE CHANGING MISSION OF COLONIAL WILLIAMSBURG— THE CASE OF RACE

Influenced by the French Annales school, the new social history became the trendiest and most influential school of historical thought emerging in the United States in the 1960s and 1970s. History was now to be less about political thought or about elite personages (especially wealthy, powerful, and educated White men) and more about everyday life as experienced by all types of people in the society, including women, Blacks, the uneducated, the sick, and the incarcerated. New topics, such as labor history, the history of education, and the history of the family became more prominent. Methods and approaches used in the social sciences, including population studies and demographics became more important. As the young new professionals completed their training in history departments and library and information science schools around the country and joined the growing ranks of the staff at Colonial Williamsburg, they brought their new perspective with them. Colonial Williamsburg might still be a paean to patriotism and the founding fathers, but it should also tell the story of other groups whose stories had so far been overlooked at Colonial Williamsburg.[54]

Let us consider the issue of race at Colonial Williamsburg.[55] Before the Second World War, the historic site at Jamestown, just down the road from Williamsburg, was not open to Blacks. Rockefeller Jr. insisted that the grounds, the houses that were open to public viewing, and the shops where craftsmen were demonstrating their trades be open to Blacks as well as Whites.[56] However, under Virginia state law, all lodging and restaurants were still segregated, including those on the Colonial Williamsburg property. When food and lodging facilities were integrated in 1951, there was some White backlash. Some shops where goods were sold by Colonial Williamsburg were also closed to Blacks before the war. Dormitories for the reenactors on the historical site were also segregated. Blacks only gained admission to the College of William & Mary in the late 1960s.

What about the portrayal of Blacks at Colonial Williamsburg? For the most part, Blacks were not mentioned in the Colonial Williamsburg literature. For example, in Foundation President William Chorley's twenty-five-year retrospective of Colonial Williamsburg, written in 1951, there was not a single mention of Blacks. Despite slightly more than half of the Williamsburg population being Black in the eighteenth century,[57] including many free Blacks, the only representations of Blacks at Colonial Williamsburg from the late 1940s to the mid-1970s was as slaves. Blacks were depicted in these portrayals as an economic asset or, for example, only as a medium to show the greatness of George Washington, who had many of his slaves saved through baptism.

Occasionally, Blacks were presented in a positive light, as providing good service, such as in their role of carriage drivers and narrators for international visitors, but nevertheless portrayed as being subservient to Whites.

The new social history that began in the 1960s only gained a firm grasp of Colonial Williamsburg in the late 1970s.[58] In 1979, Dennis O'Toole (deputy director of museum operations) and Shomer Zwelling (research historian) pushed for change. A conference held that same year was the first step toward integrating the full range of African American activities into the story told by Colonial Williamsburg. In summer 1979, six Black college students were hired for the summer, and they portrayed both slave and free men. In 1980, a Black Music program was started.[59] The following year, an evening program called African Traditions was initiated as was "The Other Half Tour" which examined the complex lives of Blacks in Colonial Williamsburg society, including issues about runaways, slave culture, and interracial relations.[60] In 1994 a mock slave auction was reenacted on the historic site, where both Whites and one free Black bid on Black slaves. This proved to be a highly controversial event, drawing coverage from numerous newspapers across the nation, including the *Washington Post* and the *New York Times*, as well as criticisms from the NAACP and the Southern Christian Leadership Conference. In 1996, Colonial Williamsburg held a conference entitled, "Interpreting the Early African-American Experience: More than Just Slavery."

By this time, the Foundation had clearly changed its programs related to Blacks—and in fact, more generally to the new social history. Nevertheless, it was sometimes difficult for Colonial Williamsburg to know how to handle Black history. At Carter's Grove, the plantation owned by Colonial Williamsburg but located six miles from the main historic site, portrayals of some aspects of slave life made visitors uncomfortable, and there was apparently some self-censorship in the topics the interpreters covered. The interpreters themselves were also sometimes uneasy. At first, watermelon was displayed prominently in the Black quarters and a watermelon garden was grown outside. However, some of the interpreters and curators were uneasy that the site was playing too much on Black stereotypes, so the next year watermelon was downplayed and other kinds of melons were planted—despite the fact that the evidence showed conclusively the prominence of watermelon in the slave diet.

AUTHENTICITY AS ABOUT EXPERIENCE RATHER THAN ABOUT FACTS

So far, we have considered the notion, pioneered by Goodwin for Colonial Williamsburg, that authenticity is about historical accuracy. In this criteria, if the buildings and the artifacts in them are either real artifacts or historically faithful reproductions, if the stories told by the interpreters or in the publications of Colonial Williamsburg are historically correct, then the historic site has achieved authenticity. We have seen that Colonial Williamsburg had set for itself a high bar with this standard and often but not completely achieved it. However, there is a thought among tourism scholars that, in an important way, authenticity at heritage sites is more about the tourist experience than it is about measuring the offerings against historical correctness. In this section, we explore this idea by examining the work of two scholars. Basing her analysis of Colonial Williamsburg on the work of phenomenologist Hermann Schmitz, the geographer Christina Kerz argues that "atmosphere" is critically important to authenticity.[61] What she means by this is that authenticity is the process of a visitor immersing herself in the atmosphere of Colonial Williamsburg, which leads to a transformation in the visitor's affective and emotional engagement. Thus, authenticity is a "rooting in place-based experience."[62] Of course, the environment itself matters as well, as does a match between the environment and the interests of the visitor: "the connotation of that felt authenticity as well as the probability to evoke this emotion can be influenced when framing the situational settings and arranging the elements of the atmospheric: the interests/desires of the audience, the interests/desires of the authors/actors in charge and the factual background of the subject matter have to be balanced for that."[63] Kerz explains the five stages in this process as she immersed herself in Colonial Williamsburg. We let her speak extensively in her own words:

Phase 1: *"And then I came over there because he seemed friendly."*

The atmospheric affects the visitors by gripping them…. There are several fields that provide such a space for atmospheric involvement. One is the realm of personal preferences that visitors find echoed in the Historic Area. Very often a sense of place that is connected to a visitor's imaginations of the past is experienced in this phase. But it is also "the other" that demands attention—and that can be anything from newborn lambs to the "live fire" from the cannon. The olfactory is another field that connects visitors to the atmospheric.

Phase 2: "Everything around just brings this sense of calm."

The second phase is best described as "becoming holistically immersed." The vital drive is gaining momentum and the visitors are opening up toward the momentary; they feel safe to "take a deep breath and go back in time." This corporeal expansion is often connected to a 'lackadaisical feeling' and to impressions of tranquility and freedom that are caused, for example, by ecstasies rooting in the sounds of the Fifes and Drums or the lack of any "loud advertisement."

Phase 3: "It is every street in America, it is your street."

In the unfolding stage, visitors experience the Historic Area as "the center of [their] universe" and are fully (caught) in the moment: "It's almost like a spiritual high." The deep immersion also makes visitors experience a sense of community when walking the main street of the Historic Area.... The intense feelings revolving around questions of identity and belonging that are atmospherically mediated here make the experiences become ever more relevant to the visitor's personal lifeworld.

Phase 4: "OK, men wear pink, I didn't think that!"

Visitors now begin to connect their experiences in the Historic Area to existing archives of emotions and knowledge: "[W]hen they say they were fighting for their freedoms, they were really fighting for their freedom! They weren't going to a ballot box, they weren't creating a Facebook page." New regimes of orientation are formed; the feelings become more permanent. Visitors are "ok with things being fuzzy." They also learn about issues one can only figure out by engaging in the atmospheric of the Historic Area.

Phase 5: "It's like I've been here all my life."

This stage marks the peak of atmospheric involvement: Colonial Williamsburg has become "like an addictive drug in a good sense." The new frameworks of emotion and knowledge become embedded into the visitor's identity and everyday life. The feeling of authenticity that has evolved is neither tied to the subject matter of the historical events or the buildings, nor is it embedded in the place itself. Rather, it is an emotion rooting in an individual's atmospheric involvement. It is a permanent situation of a state that has become detached from any place-based situations of a current moment: It just feels like home. And it has nothing to do with coming here and "Oh, look at all the history." With me it goes beyond that: it's an actual love for the place, just because it is what it is. And getting outside the colonial area into town, I carry that feeling with me.

Archivist Marina Mayne also latches on to the importance of an immersive experience as the key to authenticity, as she conducted an empirical analysis of three living history museums: Colonial Williamsburg, Greenfield Village, and Conner Prairie.[64] She notes that: "Many staff across sites described that an authentic experience meant an immersive experience: immersed in the time period, a sense of the past, or stories of the site, that could also be a subconscious experience."

Her particular interest was in understanding the role of objects in creating this immersive experience. As she notes, the individual objects themselves are not the point, but rather it is what they contribute to an overall experience: "when objects are chosen, their [sic] very much chosen as an assemblage.... It's not about an individual object.... The object in itself is kind of the center of the web that kind of spread out to all these [connections]. The object is one piece of building an authentic experience."[65]

Mayne notes a change in curatorial objectives at Colonial Williamsburg—"towards valuing what the objects do, instead of what they are." In this respect, reproductions can be more valuable than original artifacts presumably because the setting can be more precisely designed using reproductions rather than what originals might be available, and because these can be less fragile and more easily replaced if damaged through the handling of many visitors. Objects can increase immersion for the visitor, Mayne argues, by their roles in telling part of the story, creating an environment, building curiosity, engaging the senses, assisting with programming, and creating connections.[66] Immersion is also more readily achieved if the visitor can be an active participant: "making connections between the past and present (visitors own lives) becomes easier for guests when they can do something, hear something, or see something (like cooking)."[67]

This change in curatorial objective at Colonial Williamsburg was part of the reaction to the social history we have explored above, and which is directly connected to the effort to help more visitors, some with different interests and changing demographic profiles, be able to relate to (/immerse themselves in) the heritage site rather than using it solely to propagate a particular patriotic message about American ideals in its early years. Mayne quotes Smithsonian Institution curator David Allison on this point: "museums like Colonial Williamsburg and Plimouth Plantation that have an overtly national or political perspective may find it more difficult to pull away from their overarching narratives to break history into easily relatable, experiential nuggets that can spark visitor's curiosities."[68]

Mayne also noted a tradeoff between authenticity and comfort, which is important to enable the visitor to immerse herself in the living history museum: "Staff want the experience to be authentic but visitors to be comfortable enough for them to be immersed. They mentioned, for example, that they don't want visitors to be worried about how uncomfortable the heat is in a room so they add air conditioning or trees for shade so visitors focus on the experience and stories."[69]

AUTHENTICITY AS A COMMODITY

Charles Alan Watkins, director of the Appalachian Cultural Museum at Appalachian State University, has told a fascinating story about the sale of Williamsburg reproduction furniture.[70] Its relevance here is that it gives insight into the commodification of authenticity and the circumlocutions that the Colonial Williamsburg Foundation took to protect authenticity as an asset.

The first building was opened to the public in Colonial Williamsburg in 1934, and it needed to be furnished—with both antiques and historically faithful reproductions. It would have been entirely consistent with the plans of the Foundation to sell this reproduction colonial furniture in its shops in Williamsburg and through selective high-end stores around the country. However, Tomlinson, a manufacturer of medium-priced furniture from North Carolina, beat the Foundation to the market. At the International Home Furnishings Market in Chicago in 1936, Tomlinson innovatively displayed a period room of colonial furniture under the name Williamsburg Galleries and offered for sale 140 different items in this collection. This display was the hit of the trade show, and Tomlinson received orders from twenty stores. This despite the fact that the furnishings had as much in common with Victorian as with colonial design.

The Colonial Williamsburg Foundation was not amused. It felt that the Foundation had branding rights to the Williamsburg name and should be the sole proprietor of this type of furniture.[71] It formed a subsidiary corporation named Williamsburg Craftsmen, which battled with Tomlinson for the next nine years. The battle only subsided at the end of the Second World War, when furnishing tastes were changing to a more modern look.

The Foundation would not assist the Tomlinson designers in making their furniture offerings more correct in their eighteenth-century details (e.g., refusing in 1938 to allow Tomlinson employees to photograph or measure the furniture on display at Colonial Williamsburg), but they did allow—even encourage—Tomlinson to use in their marketing the phrase "design inspired by pieces in Williamsburg." The president of the Foundation had a meeting in New York City with Tomlinson executives in which he argued that Tomlinson's new product line "mis-represents the Williamsburg Restoration, injures our reputation, impedes our educational program, and actually or by implication misleads the public."[72] They also ran an advertisement disavowing their connection with Tomlinson and announced plans for their own line of reproduction furniture.

The Foundation was not only upset that they had competition in the reproduction market and that Tomlinson was first to market, they were also upset about the quality. They felt that Tomlinson was diminishing the luster of the Williamsburg brand name with its mid-priced furniture. This worry was confirmed when Baker, the well-known, high-end furniture maker, refused to make reproductions on the Foundation's behalf because they thought that Tomlinson had already firmly affiliated the Williamsburg name with mid-priced rather than high-end furniture. Williamsburg Craftsman (Colonial Williamsburg's furniture company) hired Frank Darling, who had made his reputation selling roller coasters, as its executive. Darling licensed Kittinger to manufacturer high-quality reproduction colonial furniture under their name, which they wholesaled to thirteen select retailers in major cities, including Marshall Field in Chicago and Jordan Marsh in Boston.[73] These retailers were only permitted to sell this reproduction furniture in special rooms that were created (at the department store's own considerable expense) to mimic the Raleigh Tavern on the Colonial Williamsburg site. Ironically, there were not good records of what Raleigh Tavern had looked like in the eighteenth century, so the image was a fabrication of twentieth-century planners at Colonial Williamsburg.

Colonial Williamsburg opened a blacksmith, metalsmith, and cabinet shop (Ayscough Shop) which had workman using eighteenth-century methods as much as possible, operated by the companies already licensed by Colonial Williamsburg to create reproductions for sale. It turned out that Kittinger could not actually produce the reproduction furniture in the Ayscough Shop and instead simply assembled small pieces of furniture whose parts had been made in the Kittinger factory. Even then, the craftsmen sent to Williamsburg by Kittinger could not complete the assembly work with eighteenth-century tools. They required electric power, a belt sander, and a spray gun—all of which were hidden from the public in a back room.

The Colonial Williamsburg furniture did not sell well. It was much more expensive than the Tomlinson furniture, even for very similar items. The thirteen department stores selling the product lines were also irritated with Colonial Williamsburg because of its strict rules about marketing and sales procedures, in addition to the high up-front cost of setting up these period showrooms. Several department stores abandoned the product line. In an effort to trade on its high reputation and acquire a competitive advantage, Colonial Williamsburg argued that its furniture was authentic, unlike Tomlinson's. This claim was hard to justify for two reasons: first, the furniture, although reproducing the fine and expensive details of the furniture found in the buildings at Colonial Williamsburg, was produced in Kittinger's factory in Buffalo, New York, using mass production techniques wherever possible; and, second, at this time Colonial Williamsburg did not have any actual furniture made or owned in eighteenth-century Williamsburg, only meticulously researched reconstructions.

HOW HAS COLONIAL WILLIAMSBURG MEASURED UP ON SCHOLARLY CRITERIA OF AUTHENTICITY?

At the end of chapter 1, we identified some theorizing by Athinodoros Chronis and Ronald Hampton regarding the authenticity of tourist heritage sites. How authentic is Colonial Williamsburg when seen through the lens of their theories?[74] These scholars note that there are two aspects of authenticity; and this chapter has addressed both of them. One aspect concerns experience, which they argue is subjective and different for each visitor to Colonial Williamsburg. The other was about historical exactitude. Much has been made in this chapter about

Goodwin's initial vision, which was to inspire and educate the visitor with the American lessons of patriotism through the retelling of the lives of the great White men of eighteenth-century Williamsburg. However, with the coming of the new social history in the 1960s and 1970s, Colonial Williamsburg broadened its mission, telling the stories of the everyday lives of many types of residents—not only great White men, but also women, freed and enslaved Blacks, tradesmen and craftsmen, the incarcerated, and others. It is hopelessly complex to try to tell the story of every aspect of life in Colonial Williamsburg, but the multiple narratives that are offered today are much richer and reach the interests of a wider audience than during the Goodwin years. In a sense, Colonial Williamsburg also tries to address the interests of those who are most interested in the finer things in life through its efforts to reconstruct the grandest buildings, the fancy gardens, and the high-quality artifacts exhibited in the two museums, which extend in both time and place beyond eighteenth-century Williamsburg.

This chapter amplifies on the theorizing of Chronis and Hampton. One of the scholars, Christina Kerz, who we have examined in this chapter, has provided much more detail about how a visitor experiences a tourist site such as Williamsburg—identifying a series of five steps in the visitor's affective and emotional engagement. Marina Maine explores how this immersive experience is heightened through the use of objects to tell a story, and the immersive experience of the tourist through active participation in the story.[75] In fact, as Maine notes, sometimes reproduction artifacts are better than originals in creating this immersive experience.

The second aspect of authenticity, according to Chronis and Hampton's theory, is more objective: whether the heritage site is correct in the artifacts it displays, the environment it creates, and the stories it tells. Not surprisingly, Colonial Williamsburg does an excellent job on this metric because of Goodwin's precept that authenticity is equivalent to historical exactitude in all things. We have argued in this chapter that this is a dangerous strategy on logical and psychological grounds, that no site can get every aspect of the historic site 100 percent correct, despite the large sums of money and large number of experts who try to do so. Importantly, even the slightest failure in historic accuracy leads to questions of overall inauthenticity.

Chronis and Hampton elaborate on this point of objective authenticity by identifying five different ways in which a historic site might be authentic. Colonial Williamsburg gets very high, if not perfect marks on these five criteria. Its objects are actual ones from the site or ones that are very close reproductions (object-related authenticity). Painstaking research has been taken to tell the stories correctly (factual authenticity) in both the publications of Colonial Williamsburg and the narrative and interactions with the public by the interpreters employed there. The people whose stories are told—the story of George Washington and in more recent times the stories of Blacks—are told accurately and placed in accurate settings (personage authenticity). Colonial Williamsburg is on the same site where the eighteenth-century town was located (locational authenticity); and the environment is recreated in largely the way the place was in the eighteenth century (contextual authenticity), for example by tearing down houses built in the nineteenth and twentieth centuries and buying adjacent land to remove the traces of industrialization and return the vistas to the pastoral landscape of the eighteenth century.

Some of the inauthenticities were created for the convenience of the tourists visiting Colonial Williamsburg, for example, having them walk streets that are paved rather than muddy and under a line of trees to lessen the effect of the summer heat. Some of the inauthenticities were caused by imperfect information. For example, there are some things about eighteenth-century meals that were never written down. A few of the inauthenticities were the result of human error. Note, that to make Colonial Williamsburg as authentic as it was, required vast sums of funding, for example, to redo hundreds of homes, buy acres of land on the outskirts of the historic site, and hire hundreds of scholars to research and skilled workers to carry out what the researchers learned. It would be completely impossible for a small heritage site, such as Lindsborg, to achieve anything approaching the authenticity of Colonial Williamsburg.

Chronis also discusses "tourism imaginaries," the mindset that enables the visitor to enact life in eighteenth-century Williamsburg. All of the elements that Chronis mentions are present in Colonial Williamsburg: There is emplaced enactment: the tourist actually walks over ground that has been walked by George Washington. The story of Williamsburg is made effective by the strong narrative that Colonial Williamsburg tells through its interpreters. The stories are given meaning by moral valuation, telling how the colonists strived for liberty and freedom and what that means for today's visitor, whether they are

Americans or from another part of the world. Finally, there is emotional attachment; the visitor can really feel what it was like to live in these times, whether as a wealthy landowner or as a slave.

There are two points covered in this chapter that are not discussed in the papers we cite by Chronis and Hampton. One concerns how the elite aesthetics that sometimes drove the actions of the Rockefellers undermined Goodwin's precept of authenticity as historical exactitude. The other point we have discussed in detail is how authenticity was turned into a commodity by Colonial Williamsburg as it was trying to market its period reproduction furniture, even though the furniture was being made off-site using modern tools. There are no doubt other lessons about authenticity to be drawn from the Colonial Williamsburg story.

NOTES

1. Pulitzer Prize-winning architecture critic Ada Louis Huxtable as quoted in Giles Waterfield, "Colonial Williamsburg: Authentic, Fake, or 1920s Dreamland?" *The Art Newspaper*, August 31, 1999, https://www.theartnewspaper.com/1999/09/01/colonial-williamsburg-authentic-fake-or-1920s-dreamland (accessed February 16, 2022).

2. W. A. R. Goodwin, to the Colonial Williamsburg Foundation, 1930, as quoted in Dennis Montgomery, *A Link Among the Days, The Life and Times of the Reverend Doctor W. A. R. Goodwin, the Father of Colonial Williamsburg* (Richmond, VA: Dietz Press, 1998). Also available as "The Far-Visioned Generosity of Mr. Rockefeller," published in the *Colonial Williamsburg Journal* (winter 2000–2001), http://www.history.org/foundation/journal/winter00_01/vision.cfm.

3. Marina H Mayne, "Rebuilding the Past: Understanding the Role of Objects in Creating Authentic Experiences for Visitors to Living History Museums" (MA thesis, museology, University of Washington, 2017).

4. On authenticity in historic houses, see Barbara Wood, "A Review of the Concept of Authenticity in Heritage, with Particular Attention to Historic Houses," *Collections: A Journal for Museum and Archives Professionals* 16, no. 1 (2020): 8–33, https://journals.sagepub.com/doi/full/10.1177/1550190620904798 (accessed March 29, 2022).

5. Virginia was much larger then than it is today. It included lands to the west that are now parts of West Virginia, Ohio, Kentucky, Indiana, Illinois, Michigan, and Wisconsin.

6. For an illustrated history of the town of Williamsburg from its founding until the early twentieth century, see "500 Lazies and 500 Crazies": *Williamsburg Before the Restoration, WPA Guide to Colonial Williamsburg*, http://

xroads.virginia.edu/~ug99/coe/wpa_guide/before.html (accessed January 25, 2022). Other works with useful information about early Williamsburg include: Williamsburg Garden Club. *A Williamsburg Scrapbook* (Richmond, VA: Dietz Printing Company, 1932); William Oliver Stevens, *Old Williamsburg and Her Neighbors* (New York: Dodd Mead and Company, 1938); Works Project Administration, *Virginia: A Guide to the Old Dominion* (New York: Oxford University Press, 1940); and George Humphrey Yetter, *Williamsburg Before and After: The Rebirth of Virginia's Colonial Capital* (Williamsburg, VA: Colonial Williamsburg Foundation, 1988).

7. See, for example, Colonial Williamsburg Foundation, *The First Twenty-Five Years* (Williamsburg, VA: Colonial Williamsburg Foundation, 1951); Philip Kopper, *Colonial Williamsburg* (New York: Harry N. Abrams, 1986); Suzanne E. Coffman, and Michael Olmert, *Official Guide to Colonial Williamsburg* (Williamsburg, VA: The Colonial Williamsburg Foundation, 2000); Jane Colihan, "Williamsburg by Ear," *American Heritage Magazine* 54, no. 1 (February/March 2003): n.p., https://web.archive.org/web/20101019000245/http://american-heritage.com/articles/magazine/ah/2003/1/2003_1_31.shtml (accessed January 25, 2022); and Anders Greenspan, *Creating Colonial Williamsburg* (Chapel Hill: University of North Carolina Press, 2020). Perhaps the most influential interpretive work about Colonial Williamsburg is Richard Handler and Eric Gable, *The New History in an Old Museum: Creating the Past at Colonial Williamsburg* (Durham: Duke University Press, 1997).

8. On Goodwin's life and work, see Dennis Montgomery, A Link Among the Days, The Life and Times of the Rev. Dr. W. A. R. Goodwin, the Father of Colonial Williamsburg (Richmond, VA: Dietz Press, 1998).

9. In a 1930 speech, Goodwin recalled his pitch to Rockefeller: "In 1926, it was our privilege to point out to him that Williamsburg was the only city celebrated in connection with pre-Revolutionary and Revolutionary events that was capable of restoration. It would be impossible to acquire a territory one mile long and a quarter of a mile wide in Boston, with Faneuil Hall as its center; or in New York, with Wall Street and Trinity church as its center; or in Philadelphia with Independence Hall as its center. Whereas, here, in Williamsburg, equally famous, there remained at least seventy colonial buildings in a town surrounded by the untouched and unmarked countryside, presenting an opportunity to create a shrine that would bear witness to the faith and the devotion and the sacrifice of the nation builders." Goodwin, July 29, 1930, Williamsburg) as quoted in *The Far-visioned Generosity of Mr. Rockefeller* (Colonial Williamsburg, 2001), https://web.archive.org/web/20161104075150/http://www.history.org/Foundation/journal/Winter00_01/vision.cfm (accessed January 25, 2022). Also see W. Goodwin, "The Restoration of Colonial Williamsburg," *National Geographic Magazine* 71 (1937): 402-43.

10. In the twenty-first century, American interest in history had diminished, and many historic sites, including Williamsburg, had reductions in visitors—leading to a more precarious financial situation, which in turn resulted in the reduction of the workforce from its high of 3,600 employees and outsourcing of some infrastructural tasks. Tickets sales peaked in the late 1980s at more than 1 million sales per year. See Jack Jacobs, "Colonial Williamsburg. President Mitchell Reiss to Step Down," *The Virginia Gazette*, June 18, 2019, https://www.dailypress.com/virginiagazette/news/va-vg-colonial-williamsburg-reiss-resigns-20190618-story.html (accessed January 25, 2022).

11. See John P. Hunter, *Link to the Past, Bridge to the Future: Colonial Williamsburg's Animals* (Colonial Williamsburg Foundation, 2015).

12. Janine E. Skerry, "To Their Destined Market: Salt-Glazed Stoneware at Colonial Williamsburg," n.d., https://static1.squarespace.com/static/58dbc83f893fc01cfcc43356/t/58ed0d893a0411e543db9398/1491930508853/icfs2008-salt-glazed-stoneware.pdf.

13. WPA Guide, "Colonial Williamsburg: The Corporate Town," https://xroads.virginia.edu/~ug99/coe/wpa_guide/wmbg500.html (accessed February 16, 2022).

14. "Ramifications: Capitalizing on the Depression, WPA Guide to Colonial Williamsburg," http://xroads.virginia.edu/~ug99/coe/wpa_guide/after.html (accessed January 22, 2022)

15. On the history of gardens in eighteenth-century Williamsburg, see Kent Brinkley and Gordon W. Chappell, *The Gardens of Colonial Williamsburg* (The Colonial Williamsburg Foundation, 1995); and Marley R. Brown and Edward A. Chappell, "Archeology and Garden Restoration at Colonial Williamsburg," *The Journal of Garden History* 17 (1997): 70–77.

16. See the detailed discussion in Alexandra F. Volpert, "Living in a History Museum: Local Perspectives on Colonial Williamsburg" (Undergraduate honors thesis, College of William & Mary, 2011), https://scholarworks.wm.edu/honorstheses/392.

17. "Reactions: Congratulations and Controversy," *WPA Guide to Colonial Williamsburg*, http://xroads.virginia.edu/~ug99/coe/wpa_guide/reactions.html (accessed January 25, 2022).

18. See, for example, Michael Kammen, *Mystic Chords of Memory* (New York: Vintage Books, 1991).

19. "A Shrine of Civil Religion, Colonial Williamsburg," http://xroads.virginia.edu/~ug99/pontius/WPA/shrine.html (accessed January 27, 2022).

20. Goodwin, see note 2.

21. W. A. R. Goodwin, "The Restoration of Colonial Williamsburg," *The Phi Beta Kappa Key* 7, no. 8 (May 1930): 514–20.

22. Goodwin, see note 2.

23. Eric Gable and Richard Handler, "After Authenticity at an American Heritage Site," *American Anthropologist* 98 (1996): 568-78. And, of course, new challenges of presentation arise for Colonial Williamsburg all the time, for example, how to deal with COVID-19, or as one article said, "What's the best kind of mask to wear with a tricorn hat?" (Vicky Hallett, "Authentic and Safe: At Tourist Sites, Masking Up Without Diluting the Experience," *The Journal*, November 27, 2020, https://www.the-journal.com/articles/authentic-and-safe/ [accessed January 27, 2020]).

24. A. C. Bossom, "Colonial Williamsburg: How Americans Handle a Restoration," *Journal of the Royal Society of Arts* 90, no. 4621 (1942): 634-44.

25. Skerry, "To Their Destined Market." For more on the earliest restoration efforts, see F. S. Lincoln, Fiske Kimball, William Graves Perry, Arthur A. Shurcliff, and Susan Higginson Nash, *The Restoration of Colonial Williamsburg in Virginia* (New York: F. W. Dodge Corp, 1935).

26. For more on furnishing Colonial Williamsburg, see Camille Wells, Interior Designs: Room Furnishings and Historical Interpretations at Colonial Williamsburg, *Southern Quarterly* 31, no. 3 (Spring 1993).

27. Bossom, "Colonial Williamsburg: How Americans Handle a Restoration."

28. John D. Rockefeller Jr. Library, Colonial Williamsburg website, https://www.colonialwilliamsburg.org/locations/john-d-rockefeller-jr-library/?from =navlearn (accessed January 25, 2022).

29. American Planning Association, "Duke of Gloucester Street: Williamsburg, VA," *Great Places in America: Streets* (2009), https://www.planning.org/greatplaces/streets/2009/dukeofgloucester.htm (accessed January 25, 2022).

30. American Planning Association, "Duke of Gloucester Street: Williamsburg, VA" (2009).

31. Eric Gable and Richard Handler, "After Authenticity at an American Heritage Site," *American Anthropologist* 98 (1996): 568-78.

32. See, for example, Jihong Kim and Bong Hee Jeon, "Restoration of a Historic Town to Commemorate National Identity: Colonial Williamsburg in the Early Twentieth Century," *Journal of Asian Architecture and Building Engineering* 11, no. 2 (2012): 245-51; Waterfield, "Colonial Williamsburg."

33. Rockefeller quoted in *Report on The Colonial Williamsburg Foundation with a Summary of the Years 1980 and 1981* (Williamsburg, VA: The Colonial Williamsburg Foundation), 6. For more on the Rockefellers, see Carlisle H. Humelsine, *Recollections of John D. Rockefeller Jr. in Williamsburg, 1926-1960* (Colonial Williamsburg Foundation, 1985); and Donald J. Gonzales, *The Rockefellers at Williamsburg: Backstage with the Founders, Restorers and World-Renowned Guests* (McLean, Virginia: EPM Publications, Inc., 1991).

34. For a discussion of this term, and who used it, see E. Gable and R. Handler, "Deep Dirt: Messing up the Past at Colonial Williamsburg," *Social Analysis: The International Journal of Social and Cultural Practice* 34 (1993): 3-16.

35. John D. Rockefeller Jr., "The Genesis of the Williamsburg Restoration, *The National Geographic Magazine* 71 (April 1937): 401.

36. Reflecting on the concept of staged authenticity, see About *Authenticity Soc* 45, 334–37 (2008).

37. The Far-visioned generosity of Mr. Rockefeller, Colonial Williamsburg, 2001, https://web.archive.org/web/20161104075150/http://www.history.org/Foundation/journal/Winter00_01/vision.cfm (accessed January 25, 2022). Just how involved Wren was with the original design of what was then called the Main Building on the William and Mary campus has open to scholarly debate. Also see the discussion in "A Shrine of Civil Religion," *Colonial Williamsburg*, http://xroads.virginia.edu/~ug99/pontius/WPA/shrine.html (accessed January 27, 2022); Anon., "The Real, the Surreal and the Dirty: Perspectives on Colonial Williamsburg, Anachronism, Authenticity and Pirate Zombies," *British Food in America* 68 (fall 2021): n.p., https://www.britishfoodinamerica.com/A-Winter-Number-Featuring-Questions-of-Authenticity/the-critical/The-real-the-surreal-and-the-dirty-Perspectives-on-Colonial-Williamsburg-anachronism-authenticity-and-pirate-zombies/#.YfG9gC-B2Kd (accessed January 26, 2022); and T. C. McDonald "The Fundamental Practice of Fieldwork at Colonial Williamsburg," *Perspectives in Vernacular Architecture* 13, no. 2 (2006): 36–53. Specifically on the Wren building reconstruction, see Carl Lounsbury, "Beaux-Arts Ideals and Colonial Reality: The Reconstruction of Williamsburg's Capitol, 1928–1934," *Journal of the Society of Architectural Historians* 49, no. 4 (December 1990): 373–89; M. Catherine Savedge, "The Wren Building at the College of William and Mary; Architectural Summary; Interior Restoration: 1967–1968," Research Report 195, Department of Architecture Research, Colonial Williamsburg (October 1969), http://research.history.org/DigitalLibrary/Viwe/index.cfm?doc=ResearchReports/RR195.xml (accessed October 15, 2018); and Suzanne Seurattan, "The Wren: You Know the Building; What About Its History?" William & Mary, December 22, 2015, https://www.wm.edu/news/stories/2015/the-wren-you-know-the-building,-but-do-you-know-its-history.php (accessed October 15, 2018).

38. See Waterfield, "Colonial Williamsburg"; Gable and Handler, "Deep Dirt"; and Anon., The Real, the Surreal and the Dirty."

39. Anders Greenspan, "A Shrine to the American Faith: Americanism and the Restoration of Colonial Williamsburg, 1926–1960" (PhD diss., history, Indiana University, May 1992).

40. On the history of the museum, see Ben Swenson. "The Eye of a Folk Art Pioneer," *Colonial Williamsburg Foundation* (Spring 2017): n.p.; Laura Pass Barry, "Abby Aldrich Rockefeller and Her Folk Art Museum," *incollect*, January 11, 2017, https://www.incollect.com/articles/abby-aldrich-rockefeller-the-woman-behind-the-museum (accessed February 10, 2022); Abby Aldrich Rockefeller Folk Art Center, *New York Graphic Society* (1981); Beatrix T.

Rumford and Carolyn J. Weekley, Treasures of American Folk Art from the Abby Aldrich Rockefeller Folk Art Center (Little, Brown in association with the Colonial Williamsburg Foundation, April 1989); and Elizabeth Stellinger, "Revisiting The Art of the Common Man," *Antiques Magazine*, January 11, 2017, http://www.themagazineantiques.com/article/revisiting-the-art-of-the -common-man/.

41. Colonial Williamsburg, "DeWitt Wallace Decorative Arts Museum," https://www.colonialwilliamsburg.org/locations/dewitt-wallace-decorative-arts -museum/ (accessed February 10, 22).

42. For more about the Wallace Museum, see Sandra G. Boodman, "Williamsburg Gets $12 Million For Mental Hospital, Museum," *The Washington Post*, April 20, 1982; and Robin Winks, *Laurance S. Rockefeller: Catalyst for Conservation* (Washington, DC: Island Press, 1997).

43. The visitors prior to the Second World War were described as wealthier, slightly older, better educated, and with fewer children than the visitors in recent years. These early visitors were more likely to be descendants of those who lived in Colonial Williamsburg or who were prominent in Virginia politics. Their interests were primarily in architecture, furnishings, and garden designs. (Greenspan, "A Shrine to the American Faith").

44. Hiram J. Herbert, "Williamsburg: The Ideal Hometown," *Better Homes and Gardens*, July 13, 1936, as cited in Elaura Highfield, *Public History and the Fractured Past: Colonial Williamsburg, the Usable Past, and the Concept of an American Identity* (MA Thesis, Middle Tennessee State University, December 2014). Also see Barbara Trigg Brown, "Williamsburg, a Shrine for American Patriots," *American Homes*, November 1, 1934.

45. There were feature articles about Colonial Williamsburg in *Architectural Digest* in 1931, 1935, and 1937. See the discussion in Luke Dunnington, *The Advertising and Marketing of Colonial Williamsburg During the Great Depression*, http://xroads.virginia.edu/~ug99/dunnington/intro.html (accessed January 27, 2022). Dunnington notes that Colonial Williamsburg got a lot of free advertising in newspapers, leading to a broad population having a familiarity with the historic site.

46. Eric Gable and Richard Handler, "After Authenticity at an American Heritage Site," *American Anthropologist* 98 (1996): 568–78.

47. Jean Anderson, *Recipes from America's Restored Villages* (New York: Ballantine Books, 1987).

48. Charlotte Turgeon, *Famous Meals from Williamsburg* (Williamsburg, VA: Colonial Williamsburg Foundation, 1982).

49. These examples come from Anon., "The Real, the Surreal, and the Dirty" For a balanced sense of the challenges of using eighteenth-century recipes today, see Alyssa Connell and Marissa Nicosia, "Cooking in the Archives: Bringing Early Modern Manuscript Recipes into a Twenty-First Century

Kitchen," http://archivejournal.net/notes/cooking-in-the-archives-bringing -early-modern-manuscript-recipes-into-a-twenty-first-century-kitchen/ (July 2015; accessed November 6, 2018).

50. This story is told in Eric Gable and Richard Handler, "After Authenticity at an American Heritage Site," *American Anthropologist* 98 (1996): 568-78.

51. Gable and Handler, "After Authenticity at an American Heritage Site."

52. Gable and Handler, "Deep Dirt."

53. Ada Louise Huxtable, *The Unreal America: Architecture and Illusion* (New York: New Press, 1997).

54. On social history, see, for example, Frederick M. Binder and David M. Reimers (eds.), *The Way We Lived: Essays and Documents in American Social History* (Boston: Cengage Learning, 2000); Miles Fairburn, *Social History: Problems, Strategies and Methods* (New York: Macmillan, 1999); James Henretta, "Social History as Lived and Written," *American Historical Review* 84 (1979): 1293-323; Christopher Lloyd, *Explanation in Social History* (Oxford, UK: Basil Blackwell, 1986); Peter N. Stearns, "Social History Today... and Tomorrow," *Journal of Social History* 10 (1976): 129-55; and Olivier Zunz (ed.), *Reliving the Past: The Worlds of Social History* (Chapel Hill: University of North Carolina Press, 1985).

55. The analysis here of race at Colonial Williamsburg relies upon the following sources: Anon., "The Real, the Surreal, and the Dirty"; "A Shrine of Civil Religion," *Colonial Williamsburg*; Volpert, "Living in a History Museum"; Highfield, *Public History and the Fractured Past*; Eric Gable, Richard Handler, and Anna Lawson, "On the Uses of Relativism: Fact, Conjecture, and Black and White Histories at Colonial Williamsburg," *American Ethnologist* 19, no. 4 (November 1992): 791-805; Ywone Edwards-Ingram, "Before 1979: African American Coachmen, Visibility, and Representation at Colonial Williamsburg," *The Public Historian* 36, no. 1 (February 2014): 9-35; Cary Carson, "Colonial Williamsburg and the Practice of Interpretive Planning in American History Museums," *The Public Historian* 20, no. 3 (summer 1998): 11-51; Greenspan, "A Shrine to the American Faith"; Nicole Carroll, "African American History at Colonial Williamsburg" (Dissertations, Theses, and Masters Projects, Department of American Studies, College of William & Mary, 1999), https://scholarworks.wm.edu/cgi/viewcontent.cgi?article=5750&=&context=etd&=&sei -redir=1&referer=https%253A%252F%252Fscholar.google.com%252Fscholar %253Fstart%253D60%2526q%253Dcolonial%252BWilliamsburg%252Band %252Bauthenticity%2526hl%253Den%2526as_sdt%253D0%252C6#search= %22colonial%20Williamsburg%20authenticity%22 (accessed February 8, 2022); and Eric Gable, "Maintaining Boundaries, or 'Mainstreaming' Black History in a White Museum," *The Sociological Review Monograph* 43, no. 2 (1996): 177-202.

56. Also, Rockefeller and his wife provided funding for a new school for Blacks in Williamsburg, which was built in 1938.

57. According to the 2010 US Census, the Black population in Williamsburg had fallen to 13 percent.

58. One exception was archeological digs to understand slave life better, which began in the late 1960s and continued for many years. An even earlier exception was the New York public relations firm, Raymond Rich Associates, which was hired in 1940 to help Colonial Williamsburg attract more visitors. Here is how the historian Cary Carson described the position of Rich: "While the consultants urged educators to make every effort "to insure [*sic*] accuracy as to historical data and its interpretation," they also encouraged them to recognize "the probable desirability of change from time to time in the selection and interpretation of facts," depending on the national issues they wanted to address. Ahead of their time, Rich Associates had figured out that outdoor museums often attract a breed of historical fundamentalists who believe that, if they can just restore and refurnish the museum's physical settings authentically, the lessons of history will teach themselves. Wrong, came back the answer from New York. Facts alone do not speak for themselves. Objective truth is chimera, historical reality consensual, interpretation selective, the practice of history revisionist, and the meanings we ascribe to the past relative and subject to change" (Carson, "Colonial Williamsburg and the Practice of Interpretive Planning in American History Museums").

59. From 1979 to 2003, Colonial Williamsburg also owned Carter's Grove, a plantation six miles from the main historic site. At Carter's Grove, one could visit slave quarters, recreated in part through archeological analysis.

60. For more information on this tour and related issues, see Anna Lawson, "'The Other Half': Making African-American History at Colonial Williamsburg" (PhD diss., University of Virginia, 1995).

61. Christina Kerz, "Atmospheres and Authenticity: The Example of Colonial Williamsburg, Virginia (USA)," *Proceedings of 3rd International Congress on Ambiances* (September 2016, Volos, Greece), 915-20. For a similar approach, see Mark Kristmanson, "The Signature of the City: Abandonment and Dreaming in Colonial Williamsburg and Ottawa," *Historia* 30, no. 1 (2011): 227-51, https://www.scielo.br/j/his/a/zmYtRZNjrFg8HZHxybcJbML/?lang=en&format=html (accessed February 18, 2022).

62. Schmitz, as quoted in Kerz, "Atmospheres and Authenticity."

63. Schmitz, as quoted in Kerz, "Atmospheres and Authenticity."

64. Mayne, "Rebuilding the Past."

65. Colonial Williamsburg staff member Peter Inker, as quoted in Mayne "Rebuilding the Past."

66. However, objects also can detract from immersion, Mayne argues, by disrupting the story, creating false assumptions about the past or present, distracting the visitor or focusing their attention on the wrong things, being

overwhelming or confusing, fetishizing objects, and reducing opportunities for hands-on experience.

67. Words of an anonymous Colonial Williamsburg staff member, as quoted in Mayne, "Rebuilding the Past."

68. As quoted in Mayne, "Rebuilding the Past."

69. Mayne, "Rebuilding the Past."

70. Charles Alan Watkins, "The Tea Table's Tale: Authenticity and Colonial Williamsburg's Early Furniture Reproduction Program," *West 86th: A Journal of Decorative Arts, Design History, and Material Culture* 21, no. 2 (fall–winter 2014).

71. The Federal Trade Commission ruled in favor of Colonial Williamsburg that Tomlinson could not use the name Williamsburg Galleries. But this occurred only in 1943, when both organizations had largely ceased reproduction furniture manufacture because of the war. Tomlinson was allowed to use the name Tomlinson Galleries—Modern Adaptations of Williamsburg Furniture.

72. Kenneth Chorley, Williamsburg Restoration president, June 29, 1936, as quoted in Watkins, "The Tea Table's Tale."

73. They also opened a salesroom in Colonial Williamsburg, Craft House.

74. Of course, many other scholars have addressed the issue of authenticity in Colonial Williamsburg. We have discussed a number of these scholars in this chapter. One that we have not discussed that is worth noting is Isabel McBryde, "The Ambiguities of Authenticity—Rock of Faith or Shifting Sands? *Conservation and Management of Archaeological Sites* 2, no. 2 (1997): 93–100.

75. One point of disagreement between Kerz and Chronis, which needs further discussion than we can provide here, is that Chronis argues that each individual visitor has their own subjective engagement, whereas Kerz argues that these individual subjective engagements can—at least to a certain degree— be transcended to show some commonalities across these various subjective engagements.

5

AUTHENTICITY IN LARGE PUBLIC HERITAGE TOURISM SITES

The Case of Gettysburg

Remove Confederate statues on the Gettysburg battle-field... monuments to states and people who left the USA to perpetuate slavery are wrong, Wrong, WRONG!

—Elizabeth Farnham, Letter to the Editor, Evening Sun, June 2020[1]

It is rather for us to be here dedicated to the great task re-maining before us—that from these honored dead we take increased devotion to that cause for which they here gave the last full measure of devotion—that we here highly re-solve that these dead shall not have died in vain; that this nation shall have a new birth of freedom; and that this government of the people, by the people, for the people, shall not perish from the earth.

—Abraham Lincoln, November 19, 1863

In 1863, in the midst of the American Civil War, two armies were moving toward a collision that led to the Battle of Gettysburg in

Pennsylvania and to its subsequent commemoration with the installation of some forty statues and markers dedicated to the Confederacy and, overall, to a national park and cemetery displaying more than 1,300 monuments and other commemorative markers. It was about these forty monuments and markers that the letter to the editor from Elizabeth Farnham complained. Her comments came in response to the rising discourse about racial inequality in the United States, most immediately to the death of George Floyd on May 25, 2020, and just barely a year before the City of Richmond—capitol of the Confederacy in the 1860s—dismantled its statue of Virginian Robert E. Lee.

Removing this statue was major news because, almost from the summer that his army had lost its fight at Gettysburg, Lee became lionized as a mythical, near saintly icon of Southern virtues and, not much later, of the Lost Cause. Farnham's letter could just as easily have been written in the 1880s or 1890s, in 1917, or in 1938 when other Confederate and Union monuments were unveiled on the battlefield. Only months after the fighting ended in 1865, these debates began. The entire United States became embroiled in a simmering debate about the significance of the battle, the Civil War, the role of slavery, states' rights, and racism in America. A Confederate flag was brought into the US Capitol Building on January 6, 2020—something that did not occur at any point during the Civil War—reminding Americans that they were still picking sides in the conflict. Gettysburg has proven, time and again, to be a flashpoint for unhealed discussions about the conflict. The vitriolic debates that ensued connected prior and current perspectives about "what really happened."

The Gettysburg story is complex and a daunting challenge for historians and students of information. The combination of complexity, volume, and variety of information and misinformation produced over more than a century of remembrance poses a great challenge as we discuss the connected issues of heritage tourism, authenticity, and misinformation.

The Gettysburg case contrasts with Lindsborg and Williamsburg along at least five dimensions: it is a much larger site; it attracts the largest number of visitors and the largest share of public interest; it has been subject to the greatest amount of historical research; it has been affiliated with the largest number of professional staff members, ranging from historians to tour guides (park rangers); and it has been deemed by politicians, historians, and the public at large as a central event in the broad expanse of American history. The focus in this chapter is not on the degree of authentic ethnicity (as in the case of Lindsborg) or on the historical authenticity of the furnishings (as in Williamsburg), but instead on the various issues related to the meaning and significance of the Civil War, almost from the time of the battle until today.

We first present basic information about the battle itself—surprisingly, still a contested narrative about exactly what occurred—and the subsequent role of President Abraham Lincoln. We then discuss the role of tourists—tens of millions of whom have traveled to Gettysburg. Next, we describe the emergence of interpretative controversies about the battle and describe how the battle remained controversial across five major themes: honoring dead heroes, the role of reconciliation, Lost Cause beliefs, the impact of violence and trauma, and the overarching contextual issue of race. We then take up how park preservation strategies, as administered by the National Park Service (NPS), responded to these various perspectives. The chapter concludes with a discussion of the implications of the Gettysburg case for understanding the nature of authenticity within the broader context of heritage sites and how American citizens (not only tourists) view this history.

We begin by establishing a baseline of settled facts about what happened. The town and vicinity of Gettysburg, where the battle took place, is located in southern Pennsylvania, approximately sixty miles northwest of Baltimore. Only eighty miles separates Gettysburg from the nation's capital—or from Virginia, which represents the northern frontier of the Confederacy. In 1863, Confederate forces under the command of Confederate General Robert E. Lee, proceeded northward in an attempt to take the two-year-old war to the North (Union), with the goal of proceeding as far as Harrisburg (the state capital of Pennsylvania and an industrial powerhouse) and possibly even to Philadelphia (then the second largest city in the United States). During the second half of June 1863, the Union marshalled forces to repel the anticipated invasion. While these facts are known, there has been considerable ongoing debate over the specific activities of both Union and Confederate forces during the three days of fighting at Gettysburg.[2]

The two armies clashed on July 1. As they realized that the engagement was upon them, both sides rushed up reinforcements, leading to multiple battles spread across three days and more than 11,000 acres of battleground. On July 4, the battle was over; Lee's army retreated southward, back into Virginia; while the Union army, exhausted, did not pursue them as conventional military practice would have called upon them to do. That failure led President Lincoln to criticize the commanding Union general, George Meade, who he had appointed as commander of these troops only a few days before the battle. Instead of being a decisive victory ending the war, as Lincoln had hoped for, the fighting continued for another two years.

Tourists began visiting the battlefield before the end of the summer of 1863. Between 1934 (when good records began to be kept) and the mid-2010s, more than 130 million people visited the park. Many American presidents made the pilgrimage to Gettysburg, including Abraham Lincoln, Woodrow Wilson, Franklin D. Roosevelt, John F. Kennedy, and Lyndon B. Johnson. Except for the recent pandemic years, over a million tourists visit the battlefield each year.[3] Today, the park is operated by the US National Park Service (NPS) and comprises six thousand acres, making it the largest heritage site in the nation.[4] The park houses more monuments and other forms of memorial ephemera than any other military park, more than 1,300 items. It also is home to a massive collection of Gettysburg-battle-specific objects, including buttons, bullets, rifles, uniforms, and cannons. The NPS holds approximately 1.2 million artifacts, papers, books, and works of art concerning the battle and the Civil War, including the largest painting in the United States.[5] If authenticity is measured in part by objects rooted in a specific era and place, Gettysburg is only outnumbered in America by the collections of the Smithsonian Institution, which cover the entirety of American history.

Study of the Civil War, and of Gettysburg in particular, have been very popular. There is no accurate accounting of the number of books published about the Civil War, but estimates range from 60,000 in the 1970s to 100,000 today. At least 6,000 books have been published about the Battle of Gettysburg alone,[6] making it the most massive literature on any military event in American history.[7] The park's Facebook account has more than 146,000 followers.

Of the surviving participants from the battle, thousands published articles and books, delivered speeches, or attended veteran events between the 1870s and the 1930s. The consensus among historians is that the number of soldiers involved in this battle was in the 150,000 to 170,000 range. As one NPS historian explains:

"America had never known a battle as large, bloody, or deadly as Gettysburg," with nearly 10,000 killed, often under horrendously brutal circumstances, while another estimated 30,000 were wounded, many living out their lives having had arms and legs amputated, experiencing PTSD, or suffering from drug addiction. Over 10,000 soldiers became prisoners of war (almost all Confederates) who were kept in prison camps run under terrible and unsanitary conditions that led to additional deaths. In short, at least 50,000 men were killed, wounded, missing or captured, and that figure did not include deaths of wounded soldiers sent home (mostly Union) to recover but did not.[8]

The little town that all these soldiers converged on—Gettysburg, Pennsylvania—was roughly the same size as modern-day Lindsborg: 2,400 souls.

Some 15,000 to 20,000 visitors came to the dedication of a military cemetery at the battlefield held in November 1863, when President Lincoln delivered his famous Gettysburg Address. Over 3,500 Union soldiers were buried at the military cemetery, plus an additional 3,000 from subsequent wars. Read Lincoln's statement in the epigraph to this chapter and you will immediately understand the challenge faced in this chapter: that he called on the entire nation (North and South) to remember this sacred piece of land and battle, which is exactly what they did from one generation to the next. Most White children who attended public school in the United States since the First World War have learned about this battle. However, the historical accuracy of what they have been taught about the war, and this battle in particular, can be called into question. Lincoln's two-minute speech at Gettysburg, for example, exists in 5 versions that he penned, and has its own myths: of having been written on the back of an envelope (false), over the course of many weeks before delivery (true), with slight modification after the fact (partially true).[9]

JUDGES OF THE GETTYSBURG EVENTS

Many constituencies have an interest in what happened at Gettysburg. As one Gettysburg Park historian explained when he assumed his duties there:

> I knew a lot about what people *think* they know about the battle—and most of it was wrong. Thus my initiation into the community involved a debunking of the myths, legends, and folklore that pervade the popular history.... The truth about Gettysburg is buried beneath layer upon layer

of flawed human memory and our attempting to fashion our past into something that makes our present a little easier to live on.

This led this park historian, John A. Latschar, later the park's superintendent, to write a clear-eyed, book-length analysis of how misinformation and outright falsehoods pervaded the nation's understanding of this heritage site.[10] He had to remind everyone that Gettysburg was a battlefield and should be treated as such, for example, resisting calls for landscaping as the land had appeared in some year other than 1863. (Gettysburg did not have shade trees planted to comfort tourists, as did Williamsburg.) Restoring the park to its look of 1863 became a priority for the NPS in the twenty-first century.[11] The plan for a Disneyland heritage park in nearby Northern Virginia, which was eventually abandoned due to the outrage of local citizens, represented a potential assault on Gettysburg's authenticity.[12] For a century, the Gettysburg park has fought and continues to fight local battles concerning encroachments by restaurants, gas stations, hotels, and tourist shops onto contiguous private land that had been part of the battlefield. NPS understood the threat to authenticity of these encroachments. This is what tourism scholar Athinodoros Chronis called "contextual authenticity," as we described in chapter 1.

A later NPS historian engaging with these battles over authenticity and misinformation, Thomas A. Desjardin, explained:

> American mythology has established Gettysburg as the greatest, biggest, most important, most heroic, most savage, bloodiest battle the nation ever fought. The hyperbole extends to the soldiers who fought there, who were the best, endured the worst, fought the hardest, and achieved for Americans a place in the pantheon of history's greatest military conflicts.... Without surviving Gettysburg, legend has it, the United States would not have survived, and with its death would have fallen the idea of global democracy. Nothing less than worldwide freedom was saved there.[13]

Southern sympathizers pointed to Gettysburg as the time when the Confederacy had "lost" its bid to be an independent nation, but nevertheless when the South ensured a lasting sense of dignity and nobility emblematic of the nation's highest moral aspirations. Whether the war had been fought over the enslavement of African Americans did not play a significant role in the discussions until recent decades.

The mythology about the battle of Gettysburg has evolved for more than a century, and has proved, especially since the 1990s, as a great challenge for historians. It is at that time that they began to pivot away from decades-long discussions about military tactics and strategies and toward a reexamination of the role of the battle and the park in commemoration and national memory, examining how the park evolved from a memorial to the soldiers to, as one historian saw it, a process of "veneration, defilement, and redefinition."[14] As late as the 1930s, veterans of the battle and their veteran organizations were still promoting the site's importance as a message of heroic noble sacrifice, while others advocated for the promotion of reconciliation between North and South. The sons and daughters of these veterans continued to promote both messages, as have tourists up until the present day.

After the Second World War, the NPS reshaped the messaging it presented to the millions of park visitors about the significance of the event presented. The NPS has operated the park since 1933 and has wielded the most influence on how the nation views the battle. NPS seeks objectivity and rues the misinformed views about Gettysburg that are held by millions. This issue has entered a new phase in the twenty-first century as the NPS revamps its messaging to proclaim the growing consensus among professional historians that the Civil War was fought over whether the South would be able to preserve slavery. The NPS has found this task extremely challenging. It is a battle over "contested memories."[15]

From the earliest days until today, tourists have believed they know what constitutes the facts of what happened at Gettysburg, and this belief has set their expectations about what is authentic. If they regard Gettysburg as a mythical sacred experience, they expect their beliefs to be confirmed by being where "it happened," to see the sacred objects that had been used in the battle itself, to be told about how "brave," "noble," and "important" the contestants were. Adopting the same pattern seen at other heritage sites, tourists often have little tolerance for historians and park rangers who deviate from their expected mythology.[16] This intolerance for views different from their own appears to be more strident in Gettysburg than in Lindsborg or even Williamsburg. This intolerance also extends to artifacts. The most insistent "Civil War buffs," as well as Union and Confederate reenactors, have denounced the types of inaccuracies shown by Lindsborg's citizens when they dress in inauthentic ethnic costumes.

HOW TOURISTS CONTRIBUTE TO DISCUSSIONS OF AUTHENTICITY

How do the many tourists to Gettysburg contribute to our understanding of the role of information and authenticity? As occurred at other heritage sites, the tour guides, veterans, and (later) park historians and academic military historians did much to shape what is known about the battle. Millions of visitors absorbed and disseminated their stories, which shaped perceived authentic appreciation of events. As we saw in chapters 1 and 2, tourists and providers of tourist services often think in terms of product features (e.g., having an historically accurate locality, or named historical participants such as Lee and Lincoln). Moreover, visitors set expectations for their experiences at heritage sites, assessing the degree to which their aspirations were met; and they identify their satisfaction at meeting those expectations with their view of the site's authenticity. Their expectations and their views on authenticity were achieved at Gettysburg by a complex of factors: their availability to roam thousands of acres where actual fighting occurred; the presence of famous American generals and politicians in the battle narratives; the presence of actual artifacts such as cannons, monuments and markers scattered throughout the park to remind and accentuate the importance of what happened; tour guides providing details (including mostly accurate accounts, debunking some false views but occasionally adding to the body of misinformation); and the presentation of the message of the site as sacred and important. Two scholars assessing the role of tourists concluded: "Again and again visitors at Gettysburg seem to connect with a legendary past and mythical narrative whose transformative power claims to be responsible for the birth of a united nation."[17] These park assets helped connect visitors with the past; and the success of the park in doing so can be seen in the large numbers of visitors and repeat visitors to the park.

The site is regarded as authentic because of the thousands of artifacts collected off the battlefield and displayed; and because of all the monuments.[18] Perceived factual authenticity was reinforced by tourists being immersed in the experience of visiting the site, touring the museum, watching the videos, and listening to park rangers present a narrative of events—even though the message delivered has evolved over the past 160 years. Tourists' high level of confidence in the facts they accepted was reinforced from one generation to the next because of the variety of the experiences they encountered. Another factor that scholars refer to is "personage authenticity," an awkward phrase that refers to tourists connecting with the participants in the battle: their ancestors, veterans and military units from their home states, famous generals, characters both real and fictional in novels and movies (e.g., *Gettysburg* [1993], which was based on the novel *Killer Angels*), and even Ken Burns' PBS series, *The Civil War*, which first aired in 1990 and is still widely regarded as authoritative by tourists, even though it contains known inaccuracies.[19]

Locational authenticity is crucial for visitors. Going to where an historical event occurred assists a visitor in visualizing what happened and reinforces their understanding of events. Bus rides to the actual sites, standing on Little Round Top, walking across the field of Pickett's Charge, and touching Civil War–era cannons spread throughout the park to conjure up battle lines and positions—all these help tourists connect to the historic events. The same occurs when one sees an object in the museum that they are informed belonged to a specific individual and was used at an exact location on the field. An original letter by a soldier, describing events, has a similar effect on visitors. And how the site looks is enormously impactful; that is why, for over a century, guardians of the battlefield have debated which trees and plants to have, whether to allow post–Civil War buildings to remain standing, and how many deer to allow to roam the grounds. Should the property look as it did in 1863, 1888, or 1933? The NPS has more frequently—and today—concluded that the landscape must look as much as it did at the time of the battle to enhance the authentic experience for visitors.[20] For over a century, the role of the site's landscaping influenced and intensified debates about commercial exploitation of the battlefield and neighboring land. The annual economic impact to Pennsylvania of the battlefield park's existence is estimated to run into many tens of millions of dollars.[21] Tourists tend to criticize commercialization, but they do not hesitate to buy T-shirts, Confederate flags, and Gettysburg-themed coffee mugs and postcards in gift shops in town and at the park's gift store.

Tourism scholars point out that the diversity of influences on the public reveals another feature of heritage site authenticity for visitors: boundaries between the real and perceived. Tourists use authenticity to facilitate their connection to what happened at Gettysburg and reinforce their perceptions of what is the truth in these events. They are prepared to suspend beliefs or deny facts in order to reinforce their own perceptions. For example, a Southerner might not accept that General Meade militarily beat General Lee, opting instead to view the battle as a heroic and important example of the South's brave men sacrificing their lives for a noble cause.[22] Reenactments of the battle, sometimes referred to as "staged authenticity," have remained popular over time. For example, there were large reenactments during the Civil War's centennial year of 1963 and again in 2013.[23]

Does it always work? No. For example, there are some cannons stamped with the date 1864—after the battle was over—and even though they were constructed with the same technologies as those used in the battle, tourists have complained about them and regarded them as inauthentic. Similarly, never-worn-out brick streets in Lindsborg and Williamsburg, as well as carefully maintained fences and gardens in Williamsburg also bring accusations of inauthenticity.

We should remember that the path to authenticity is shaped and reshaped over time, and in the words of tourism scholars, "negotiated" within the context of one's own worldviews and current realities. The veteran who lost an arm at Gettysburg may think differently from his grandson visiting the battlefield in the 1930s, or from a busload of high school students from his hometown in the 1990s. Changing standards of what constitutes authenticity is a further complication. Movies, as well as recent public discourse over race, affect what people believe and shape the standards by which they understand the authenticity of a tourist heritage site.

SETTLED FACTS AND NEW CONTROVERSIES

All battles are, by their nature, chaotic and noisy. They occur in unanticipated ways, and plans are discarded in the course of action. Battles, particularly large ones such as Gettysburg, are consequently difficult to deconstruct with precision afterwards. First-person accounts are problematic. The participants themselves are understandably confused and sometimes forgetful about the details, both then and later, due to the rush of adrenaline, the need to focus on their own safety, the chaos around them, and the shock of seeing the injury and death of their friends and colleagues close by. In retrospect, the truth is open to question as the participants attempt to rationalize their roles, their successes or failures, and those of their companies and armies. The uncertainty about events proved to be widespread, and often involved conflicting claims and sometimes even impossibilities. It is hard for the tourist to recreate this way of feeling, thinking, and understanding years later, outside the heat of battle. The reconstructions of both the battle participants and the tourists contribute to the creation of mythologies about what happened during those summer days in 1863. We discuss those mythologies in detail below.

The rough outline of which battles occurred, and where, were generally agreed upon by the end of the nineteenth century, although this was complicated by the large number of people on the battlefield and the simultaneous engagements in multiple locations. Specific actions and locations, with their particular topographies, were identified, and actions were catalogued with names such as the battle of Herr Ridge or Seminary Ridge during the first two days of fighting, as well as the famous "Pickett's Charge" across an open field on the third day, which resulted in six thousand Confederate casualties in less than an hour and the concomitant Confederate retreat to Virginia.[24] Nevertheless, almost every detail of what happened on those three days became the subject of controversy, misinformation, hyperbole, and honestly failed recollections. It was not uncommon for veterans on both sides to recall or relate accounts differently, even concerning small details and tiny skirmishes. But this was especially true of the larger engagements, such as Pickett's Charge.[25] These controversies persisted for many years, for example in determining the number of casualties (perhaps fifty-seven thousand) as well as the percentages of Union (perhaps 27 percent) and Confederate (perhaps 37 percent) soldiers wounded, killed, or missing at Gettysburg.[26]

Another widely studied but now largely settled debate has involved multiple related issues: the creation of a military cemetery to replace haphazardly dug shallow graves, the establishment of the park, its administration by the War Department and later the National Park Service, and the speech by President Lincoln at the cemetery's dedication. The significance bestowed upon these events has changed over time.[27] As one scholar explained: "When Americans emerged from this horrible conflict they tried to make sense of the destruction. However, they also celebrated and honored their achievements."[28]

One other settled fact is that although the battle has variously been regarded as the "High Water Mark" of Southern military activity, and as a "turning point" in the war, the rebellion continued for nearly two more years before the Confederacy collapsed in spring 1865. As late as fall 1864—over a year after Gettysburg—the outcome of the war remained in question. Many believed Lincoln would lose his bid for reelection to the presidency because of public perception that the war was unwinnable and that it kept dragging along. Some politicians and newspaper editors called for a negotiated peace, despite Lee's retreat from Gettysburg. It took additional Union military victories to successfully boost Lincoln's reelection prospects, most significantly General Sherman's capture of Atlanta just prior to the election. However, in hindsight, historians have determined that the Union success at Gettysburg, coupled with the fall of Vicksburg the following day and subsequent Confederate concentrations along the Mississippi River the following week, sealed the fate of the Confederacy.

Historians label the myth of the "High Water Mark" of the Confederacy as the core of all Gettysburg myths. A specific spot was identified at the park, called The Angle, where this event occurred; and this became what one historian described as a "must see" attraction. The spot became "littered with monuments, markers, cannons, and interpretative signs."[29]

ENDURING MYTHS AND MISINFORMATION ABOUT THE BATTLE

We now turn to myths about Gettysburg. Some of them have had a staying power of more than a century. In this section, we categorize the most common of these myths. Their survivability can be explained by the variety and number of myth-builders, generation after generation. They include, for example, early ill-informed tour guides and civil war buffs; as well as textbook writers for school children, who became teachers and tourists accepting and repeating falsehoods in the absence of accurate facts.[30]

Table 5.1 identifies the most prevalent myths concerning Gettysburg. Note that the number and variety of these myths identified were far greater than those about Lindsborg or Williamsburg. The Gettysburg myths share several common features. Each one comes in multiple forms. Each has been debated for decades. Each is rooted in the kinds of attributes one thinks required for the imprimatur of authenticity: specific locations, artifacts, buildings, participant experiences, and reports of observers.

Table 5.1   Common Myths Regarding the Battle of Gettysburg and the Gettysburg Address

Myth	Why	Authenticity Type
Battle fought over Confederates wanting shoes	*No shoe factory in Gettysburg*	*Object related, factual falsehood*
First-day fighting was minor	Battle involved 50,000 with 16,000 killed	Factual errors
Pickett's charge largest, most decisive of the war	Not the largest, most decisive, or most consequential; war lasted two more years	Factual, contextual
Photograph of dead sharpshooter	Dramatic 1860s image of soldier obviously moved to make a good image, wrong rifle for a sharpshooter	Factual, locational both inaccurate
Little Round Top fighting most important combat of the battle	Historians refute its size and significance	Factual—even participants disagreed on what occurred
Lincoln finished writing his Gettysburg Address quickly on the back of an envelope	He wrote it over several weeks, polishing just before delivering it	Factual, personage
Gettysburg is haunted with ghosts	Stories not proven but around for over a century	Locational, contextual because so many believed it
Most important battle fought in "sleepy" Gettysburg	Because it was small, but it had two colleges, forty-four businesses, ten roads, Underground Railroad stop	Locational, contextual because people believe small towns are "sleepy"
Armies met accidently at Gettysburg	Differing accounts of initial clashes	Locational, personage with commanders explaining both sides headed purposefully to the region
Abner Doubleday, a Union officer, invented baseball	Never had anything to do with its invention	Personage with others having developed the sport
Position of horses' hooves on memorials indicated if the rider was killed, wounded, or survived unscathed	Rumored to be a "code" for monument designers	Object, no such code existed, spread by early tour guides in nineteenth century

(Continued)

Table 5.1 (Continued)

Myth	Why	Authenticity Type
Battle fought over Confederates wanting shoes	*No shoe factory in Gettysburg*	*Object related, factual falsehood*
General Meade failed at Gettysburg to pursue and defeat Lee. Many additional tactual and strategic false rumors about Meade's and Lee's intents spread	Lee was quickly hailed as a noble, brilliant commander, Meade as incompetent, weak, indecisive	Factual personage. Meade won the battle, Lee lost, but Lincoln blamed Meade for not pursuing retreating Confederate army. Meade executed decisions and actions in professionally correct ways
Immigrant soldiers would not fight	Bigotry against German and Irish immigrants flooding into United States in the 1840s and 1850s	Contextual, but German and Irish immigrants were the largest foreign contingents, and their regiments performed well and took many casualties documented by historians
General Longstreet lost the battle, not Lee	Poor intelligence for both, with Lee issuing specific orders for what to do	Locational, personage as neither general fully understood where and what battle conditions existed as they took actions and made decisions

HOW THE BATTLE BECAME CONTROVERSIAL

The list of topics in table 5.1 is long, but we can focus on five myths that especially inform us about authenticity and misinformation: the roles of honoring dead heroes, desire for reconciliation, beliefs in the Lost Cause, role of violence and trauma, and the broad contextual issue of race. Each of these topics involved large constituencies engaging in discussions about truth and authenticity, even when they typically did not use the word "authentic." Each of these discussions is long-lived, in some cases lasting 160 years, from the time of the battle to the present day. There is a religious fervor associated with these myths—by veterans of both sides, early visitors, others who regarded their visits as pilgrimages, and tourists with expectations that they could affirm and learn about "what happened here" on "sacred soil." While we describe them separately, these five myths are often commingled and conflated by those who believe them. The myths concerning violence and race promise to sustain discussions about battlefield authenticity for decades—especially because some of people regard as inflammatory the NPS's current interpretation of events as displayed in its new museum opened in 2008; or by how the park rangers (at both Gettysburg and other national parks) today tell the histories of the battle, Lincoln's address, and the war. Each of these five issues generally concerns the Civil War, not just specifics of Gettysburg.

Honoring Dead Heroes

The honoring of dead heroes was a process that was made concrete—first for Union soldiers, later for Confederate soldiers—with the establishment of the military cemetery in Gettysburg in 1863. The Gettysburg Battlefield Memorial Association (GBMA) was formed the following year and began to acquire battlefield land set aside for both the cemetery and commemorative purposes. Visitors had already begun to arrive to tour the battle site. Travel guides, historical narratives, and rituals soon appeared. By the 1880s, construction of monuments was well underway, and hundreds of them were erected prior to the First World War.

One of the first individuals to articulate an interpretation was John Badger Bachelder, a portrait and landscape painter, who published one of the earliest guides to the battle, extensively interviewed veterans, and gave talks. He spent years collecting facts and anecdotes for a history that he never wrote. But in the process, he developed a framework for explaining the chronology and locations of events, which veterans responded to at his request—to situate their role within his construct. They accepted his framework, even though it was never fully accurate (perhaps because he developed it before having sufficient facts), and they reified this framework as they attached their personal histories to it.[31]

Veterans admitted their recollections were not precise. Abner Doubleday, although he did not invent baseball, contrary to widespread belief, did play an important role in the battle. He wrote to Bachelder in 1885 that, "It is difficult in the excitement of battle to see every thing going on around us for each has his own part to play and that absorbs his attention to the exclusion of every thing else. People are very much mistaken when they suppose because a man is in a battle, he knows all about it."[32] This is an important observation. Doubleday was not the only veteran to admit as much. Yet, for a half century, participants advanced their perspectives over such a long period of time that the misinformation (intentional or otherwise) in their narratives about Gettysburg became accepted common knowledge.

Bachelder's ongoing efforts had the decisive effect of making Gettysburg the premier—indeed, pivotal—battlefield of the war in the public's mind. Funded generously in his work by the US government, he could promote Gettysburg far beyond what others were doing at other battlefield sites. When he died in 1893, he had still not finished his book; and, in fact, he acknowledged there were too many conflicting perspectives and facts to settle on one story line.

Into the 1920s the narrative about Gettysburg was dominated by veterans of the war. The many memoirs and military and regimental histories they wrote celebrated the heroic deeds of all involved. Religious language appeared frequently in these accounts, as they described the site as holy, a shrine, and a "rocky citadel." Monuments erected in this time period reinforced this message. The veterans addressed the rhetoric of sacrifice and celebrated the brave activities of the soldiers. Each monument was opened with ceremony, prayer, and speeches. For example, at the dedication of the monument to the Eighty-Fourth New York troops on October 19, 1887, a speaker declared: "this monument tells you of men who were not afraid to die... of men who were not afraid to live, robbed of their health, crippled in limb... God grant that the record of your deeds may inspire us and all your fellow citizens to a patriotic devotion to the country we all love so well."[33] Monuments showed more than generals on horseback, they also displayed men dying in the arms of compatriots while carrying forward their country's flag. The monument dedicated to Georgia's Confederates had chiseled into it the words, "We sleep here in obedience to law. When duty called, we came. When country called, we died."[34] Florida's monument reminded visitors that its soldiers, "fought with courage and devotion for the ideals in which they believed," while Tennessee's "died for their convictions."[35] By the late 1880s, there was an awakening interest in the Old Confederacy to erect monuments to "commemorate the heroism of soldiers here."[36]

Forty-two thousand veterans and fifty thousand others showed up at the fiftieth anniversary ceremony of the battle, and President Woodrow Wilson delivered a speech focused on peace, honor, and reconciliation. By then, reconciliation was in the air. Each side, both Union and Confederate, felt compelled to develop an ideology—a rationale for what happened there in the Civil War—and a vestige of these rationales can still be seen today. The Confederate "ideology is characterized by explanations and justifications connected to the causes, conduct, and consequences of the Civil War that portray the Confederacy in a distinctly positive light." Union forces were presented as defending the unity of the nation.[37] These were political messages, but they were also comforting rationale for families whose men died in the war, buried in "hallowed ground"—a phrase still used today by tour guides and in battlefield signage.

As one historian observed about this era that lasted into the 1920s, the battlefield park at Gettysburg "is now a constructed view of a certain version of the past, rather than a factual depiction of some historical truth."[38] The messaging from this time served several purposes: "[it was] partially intended to resolve the tension between the expectations and the realities of wartime death... [but also] sought to imbue the tragic loss of so many with authentic meaning while helping to define an appropriate relationship between the dead and the living within a negotiated framework of remembrance and commemoration." [39]

It was challenging for the nation, and especially for the veterans and their families, to refute a narrative literally chipped into stone and cast into bronze. These narratives about heroism, nobility of soldiers, national purpose, and reconciliation were the perceived wisdom for

Figure 5.1 In 1913, Confederate and Union veterans of the Battle of Gettysburg convened a reunion. This photograph of them shaking hands over a wall where Pickett's Charge took place symbolized the message of reconciliation promoted by veterans and the National Park Service at that time, a theme that had pervaded discussions about the battle since the 1880s and that lingered into the twenty-first century. *Source:* Library of Congress, LC-DIG-ppmsca-58372.

many decades. Southerners shared that purpose but built upon it narratives of reconciliation and of the Lost Cause.

Reconciliation

Contemporaneous to the messaging about the heroism of the soldiers at Gettysburg was the theme of reconciliation among the combatants. Without denying the ferocity of the combat and the emotional peaks the soldiers experienced during the war, these elements were downplayed over the years to such an extent that historians of the late twentieth century were able to rebalance those facets to provide a more accurate accounting of the war.[40] At the fiftieth anniversary commemoration of the battle in 1913, a photograph was taken in which the Confederates who participated in Pickett's Charge were shown with their Union adversaries, the elderly Union veterans on the left and equally old Confederate veterans on the right respectfully shaking hands in a line on either side of a rock wall (see figure 5.1). The image became such an iconic representation of reconciliation that the same handshaking event was restaged and filmed at the final Civil War reunion in 1938.[41]

Union veterans began promoting the concept of reconciliation in the 1870s through their largest organization, the Grand Army of the Republic (GAR), founded in 1866.[42] They hosted or participated in commemorative anniversary events at major battlefields, including Gettysburg. Confederate veterans began participating in considerable numbers by the early 1890s. Both sides were increasingly regarded as holding sincere commitments to their causes. Commemorations came to dominate thinking about the war, discounting divisions between the two sides and avoiding discussions about slavery as the war's cause. Veterans on both sides focused on their mutual military experiences.[43] Commemorating the nobility of their causes and heroic behaviors in battle became, in the words of one historian, "nationally pervasive," conditioning the public to think less about the realities of violent war and instead to embrace a less contentious view of the past. Tourists and battlefield guides helped to structure "a shared public memory of the Civil War."[44] As a result, Lee's reputation improved dramatically, his military failure at Gettysburg sidelined. This in part was driven by his magnanimity in defeat, fostering his reputation for personal integrity—even among Union veterans—and his remaking as an authentic American patriot.

Southerners wanted to be seen as authentically patriotic and used reconciliatory events and narratives as a path to that objective. They embraced the nobility and legitimacy of what they had stood for. One in four Southern men between the ages of sixteen and forty-five had died or been wounded in the war, over half the value of the South's assets had been destroyed (farms, homes, businesses, machinery, livestock), and their largest economic asset (four million slaves) had been set free. As one historian noted, what the South did was "to become part of the national text of the remembered nation," which called for both sides "to bring hope, consolation, and patriotic pride to the once dishonored South," the act of "commemorating defeat."[45]

Lost Cause

While the Union veteran organization, the GAR, began the process of commemoration at battlefield sites, Southern veterans, newspaper editors, politicians, and especially women, created in 1866 a narrative embraced by White residents across the South, later in the North, called the "Lost Cause." It argued that the war was not primarily about slavery but instead about just and heroic sentiments. It was a rationalization of Southern sacrifice. By the late twentieth century, historians were protesting that this narrative was inauthentic. In the early twenty-first century, the American public started calling for a revisionist understanding of the fighting at Gettysburg and other battlefields, and for dismantling of equestrian statues of Southern generals in places such as Charlottesville and Richmond, Virginia. This contradicted the thesis of the Lost Cause that millions of tourists had accepted as they experienced Civil War battlefield parks.

In front of the Courthouse or on the main town square in many Southern towns one can find a statue of a Confederate soldier on an elegant stone pedestal, looking forward, leaning on his rifle. These statues were erected between the 1880s and the First World War, almost always as the result of fundraising initiatives led by women's organizations—by the spouses, widows, siblings, and children of Confederate veterans. This commemorative statuary continued to stand even in the face of African American complaints that these statues celebrate a time of slavery as well as the Jim Crow racist practices that followed the war. At the dedication ceremonies for these statues, speeches extolled the virtues of Southern veterans, with those old soldiers present often wearing ragged uniforms and displaying their medals. Boy scouts participated, as did veteran organizations of subsequent wars. Engraved in the stone pedestals were the names of local fallen Confederates.

The "Lost Cause" was the South's justification for going to war and the rationale for why it lost. The Southern Historical Society (founded in 1869), United Confederate Veterans (1889), Sons of Confederate Veterans (1896), the United Daughters of the Confederacy (1894), and other organizations promoted the Lost Cause thesis. Core to their idea was, in the words of one historian, "an intricate negotiation" between Southern and Northern communities to create "a public memory of the war's outcome in which the former Confederacy and the entire reunited nation was to find deliverance"; and that, although defeated, it did not mean that Southerners were prepared to embrace a Northern view of how society should be structured or a belief in "racial equality."[46] The well-known historian David Blight labeled it "a racial ideology" and as "the base of Jim Crow America." In fact, Southerners resisted Reconstruction and instead promoted the concept of "states' rights" as the principal reason for why they went to war with the North in 1861. Southern states repeatedly used the narrative as a mechanism for justifying their resistance to the federal government's interference in their activities.[47] Focusing more on the emotional than the political aspects, one scholar noted:

> The Legend of the Lost Cause began as mostly a literary expression of the despair of a bitter, defeated people over a lost identity. It was a landscape dotted with figures drawn mainly out of the past: the chivalric planter; the magnolia-scented Southern belle; the good, gray Confederate veteran, once a knight of the field and saddle; and obliging old Uncle Remus. All these, while quickly enveloped in a golden haze, became very real to the people of the South, who found the symbols useful in the reconstituting of their shattered civilization. They perpetuated the ideals of the Old South and brought a sense of comfort to the New.[48]

Slavery remained the under-acknowledged elephant in the room.

There is a long history of state's rights arguments from the South, including the battles over voting rights for African Americans in the 1960s. These arguments continue to be heard today. The desire for Southern autonomy to manage its society by its own rules in the post-Reconstruction era was positioned as an extension of the South's desire for autonomy originating in the American Revolution, during which

North and South fought for independence against British oppression. The Confederacy's defeat in 1865 was presented not as disgraceful but instead as in the spirit of the Revolutionaries of the 1770s, many of whose leaders were from the South, including George Washington, James Madison, and Thomas Jefferson. White male masculinity was on display in the 1860s as much as it had been in the 1770s, thus worthy of respect and commemoration. In short, the Lost Cause became the mega-myth of the Civil War manifested regularly at commemorative occasions held at Gettysburg and other military sites, regardless of who "won" on the field of battle.

The Lost Cause thesis held emphatically that slavery was *not* the reason for secession, even though historians have conclusively demonstrated the exact opposite. Southerners spoke of cultural differences, disagreements about tariff legislation, incompatibility between the agricultural economy of the South and the industrial economy of the North, and states' rights. When slavery came into discussions, the Lost Cause advocates positioned it as "humane" and suitable, given the "nature of the African Americans themselves." Many Northerners and Southerners at mid-nineteenth century shared the belief that Blacks could not succeed on their own in a White society. Historians later demonstrated that this claim was also false, pointing to examples of free African Americans living in Northern states. Despite these inconvenient facts, the Lost Cause narrative portrayed Southern African Americans as "faithful slaves," or as "happy darky stereotypes." The movie *Gone with the Wind* (1939) epitomized the Lost Cause in Homeric terms, as American mythology writ large. A year does not go by without this movie being aired on American television. It took the Civil Rights movement after the Second World War to directly challenge these notions and, as we discuss below, with the assistance of the NPS and historians at battlefield parks and Northern university history departments. The Lost Cause ethos spoke of slavery as morally superior to the harsh capitalist life of "free" white workers in the North. Ultimately, argued many Southerners, the Southern political economy would have evolved out of slavery.[49]

As a result of the Lost Cause thesis, establishing monuments to Confederate soldiers at battlefields came to communicate "a legitimacy that is widely acknowledged as appropriate and authentic."[50] As one historian observed, monuments "exert a powerful force within the interpretive text of battlefield monumentation and public memory that bears witness to the legitimization of the myth of the Lost Cause and its tacit assertion of vindication for those that fought for the cause of the South."[51] He concluded that the Lost Cause "can be described as little more than the convergence on a number of myths,"[52] which, given our analysis of the role of Civil War's characterization of authenticity, makes sense, but that nonetheless remained for millions of tourists a comprehensive and influential benchmark of what constituted authentic appreciation of what happened during the Civil War.

Academic historians and others working for the NPS battled against the Lost Cause thesis after the Second World War. For example, David Blight argued that the Lost Cause message was a successful means for the South to get past Reconstruction.[53] As late at 2021, the thesis continued to distort American politics, as ex-president Donald Trump's supporters touted its main points, especially those notions regarding White supremacy and racial anxieties—both of which still confronted NPS park historians and tour guides at Gettysburg. For example, when the park began in the 1990s to assess the messaging (in anticipation of building a new museum and visitor center), its management encountered objections to diminishing recognition of the "Lost Cause." Sons of Confederate Veterans (the organization still existed!) accused park historians of opining rather than staying with the facts of what happened. A park historian accused this organization of not realizing, "that the history of Gettysburg is little more than opinion" and noted "the many ideas put forward to explain Southern defeat."[54]

Violence and Trauma

Every issue discussed so far affecting the nation's varied perspectives of what constituted an authentic experience with Gettysburg rested on explanations and expectations that had endured for more than a century. That one still encounters the rhetoric of the Civil War even in today's politics indicates that the process of resolving identities, memories, and misinformation is still underway. Two issues, however, are only of more recent origin: explaining to the public how violent the conflict had been, and the role racism played across the entire conversation about the war. Both issues have played an important role in how the NPS explained the Gettysburg experience. Both reinforce the notion that the public understanding of Gettysburg continues to evolve.

We have already remarked upon how bloody the war was, at a time when medical practices were pitifully inadequate and new, more deadly weapons were put into use. How did this affect the national psyche? Even as the nation moved to narratives of reconciliation, it ignored uncomfortable truths, such as the violence and trauma of the civil war. The public, politicians, and veterans were all complicit in setting aside these issues. After the NPS assumed management of Gettysburg in 1933, it posted signage throughout the park that emphasized patriotic and reconciliatory messages, remaining silent on the themes of violence and trauma. Although, over the past half century, historians have documented the brutality of the war, their findings did not find their way into the plaques or statuary at Gettysburg or other Civil War battlefield parks.

Soldiers wrote letters and kept diaries that described violence. Military historians often illustrated their monographs with photographs taken soon after the battle showing the aftermath of violence. However, many regimental histories left out descriptions of the killing and wounding of the enemy. One historian spoke of the "many" who "returned in precarious physical condition," which made their reintegration into civilian life challenging.[55] Connections between the experiences of Civil War soldiers to soldiers from the First and Second World Wars, and from the Vietnam conflict, provided insights into the widespread trauma; and there was a dawning realization that the psychological effects of Civil War combat needed to be acknowledged.[56] For example, Brent Nosworthy's study of the effect of military ordnance provided insight into the violent experiences of Civil War soldiers.[57] But most histories of the Civil War, and specifically those about Gettysburg, did not address this topic, declaring instead that after the war soldiers returned home to quietly live out their lives, confident of their having carried out their duties. One student of the violence was blunt: "this assertion is simply not true."[58]

Violence is another example of a theme omitted or subjected to misinformation in the park's heritage. The NPS historians at Gettysburg and other battlefield sites were aware of this historiography and debated how to reflect these findings in their narratives and especially in signage designed to provide tourists with a "realistic" description of what happened. Planners for the Gettysburg Park in the 1980s and 1990s tried to follow the fine line of informing visitors of the violence of the battle on what now seemed to be a pastoral setting, while not dwelling on the morbid details. As one historian described: "Understanding the horrific experiences of the soldier in combat is a vital part of that history, but [it] can function as just one component of a larger interpretive experience."[59] The reality of Gettysburg was that death was a "constant companion" from a combination of combat injuries, disease, miserable weather, and bad food. As soldiers in all wars exclaim, death and injuries are happenstance events of chance and are unfair, yet they weighed on everyone's mind. Many people were willing to set aside these uncomfortable thoughts and focus instead on more palatable ideas of reconciliation and the virtues associated with the Lost Cause. Only in the 1990s, and then gingerly, did the park signage begin to include details about the violence. Instead, the most essential message delivered at Gettysburg and at other NPS sites was of a nation triumphant in reuniting itself as the ultimate legacy of this war.

Race

The final issue—slavery—is a far more contested one, with a direct bearing on authenticity. For decades, generations of managers and tour guides in military parks avoided the topics of race and slavery, often avoiding the questions or responding inaccurately to questions posed by visitors. Only in 2000, did Congress mandate that the role of emancipation had to be presented as the primary cause of the Civil War. At Gettysburg, the change only occurred fully in 2008, with the opening of a new museum and visitor center at the park. Unsurprisingly, that event generated complaints from some visitors that slavery was not the cause of the Civil War and that the NPS was misleading the public (contrary to the views of most recent historians). While racism was shown against various immigrant groups, it was most acutely directed at African Americans. This was especially true in the South during the nineteenth century. Attempts to disentangle African Americans from the nation's history have repeatedly failed; most recently, the *1619 Project* has placed race front and center in discussions about American history.[60]

African Americans have paid less attention to the Battle of Gettysburg than Whites; the number who visit the park has remained far lower than for White Americans. Blacks have questioned the relevance of the Gettysburg story: the stories about Blacks fighting in this war were untold;[61] the battle did not end the war; and the war itself did not end racism, but instead marked the beginning of the long period of Jim Crow activities. Confederates fought to preserve the enslavement of Blacks in forced work camps, elegantly called "plantations," and Union forces inadvertently facilitated post-war suppression of the ex-slaves by agreeing to end Reconstruction in 1876. Misinformation about African Americans proliferated and resisted correction into modern times. At the centennial celebrations at Gettysburg in 1963, park and community staffs intentionally avoided discussing racial issues, focusing instead on reconciliation. Southern governors touted states' rights, while northern governors portrayed an overly rosy picture of progress being made in the current civil rights movement. The African American press ignored the celebration, denying the anniversary any sense of legitimacy.[62] The centennial of the war became a lost opportunity to integrate African American experiences into the conversation about the Civil War. As David Blight noted, White Americans treated the war as "mere pageantry," which involved looking at the conflict through a sentimental gaze, clearly regarded as inauthentic by African Americans.[63]

African Americans fought in Union military units, but their story remained almost invisible in the histories of the Civil War until the late twentieth century. An estimated 179,000 Black men served in the Union Army (10 percent of its entire force), while an additional 19,000 served in the Union Navy.[64] African American residents in Gettysburg (part of free Pennsylvania) and nearby communities fled, fearing the Confederates would enslave them. Only in 2020 did the NPS present information about the fleeing of Blacks from Gettysburg.[65] Even then, the NPS did not mention the capture of hundreds of free Blacks by the Confederate forces, as General Lee marched through Maryland into Pennsylvania and retreated after the battle to Virginia. [66]

Lincoln issued the Emancipation Proclamation in 1862 as a means to deprive the Confederacy of a labor pool—a military necessity—not out of some idealistic aspiration to emancipate oppressed humans. Readers may be shocked to know that this was Lincoln's reason. While he decried slavery as a cruel system, he did not believe in Blacks' equality to Whites. Reconstruction ended with the return of the Confederate states into the Union in exchange for allowing them to politically administer their own regions, which resulted in indirect and direct suppression of the newly enfranchised African Americans. As one advocate for African Americans being fully integrated into the fabric of American history explained, "It is Black Americans who have consistently made the case that "all men are created equal."[67] It was time to reverse what historian David Blight called the nation's White-centric "segregated memory of its Civil War in Southern terms." In the process, the nation had somehow reunited, but as he phrased it, "both used and trumped race."[68] He reminded readers that although reunion was a triumph for post-Civil War America, "it could not have been achieved without the resubjugation of many of those people whom the war had freed," which led to "the tragedy lingering on the margins of American history into the twentieth century.[69]

Because the Gettysburg story as told into the early 2000s disregarded African American issues, Blacks regarded the accepted story as inauthentic and irrelevant to them—and this viewpoint no doubt continues today. That African American troops did not engage in the battle could be cited as a reason. However, as historians pointed out, the role of Black soldiers was minimized at various commemorative events around the country for the prior 150 years.[70] Ignoring African Americans had long facilitated reconciliation. One historian explained, "As a place where whites might mingle as a privileged group sharing pride in white accomplishment and propriety, Gettysburg was a unifying force." Even reenactments—a relatively new activity at this park—assisted its transformation "into a rescripted memory where slavery is absent in a sanitized landscape."[71] White male visitors and their families proportionally constituted the largest group of visitors to the battlefield, despite attempts by the NPS to broaden the site's appeal. To quote a student of the NPS: "The current focus on authenticity has discounted the importance of race in the causes and legacies of the Civil War, making African Americans feel less welcome at the shrine and in the nation's memory."[72]

HOW PRESERVATION STRATEGIES AND PARK INTERPRETATIONS AFFECTED AUTHENTICITY

The NPS has communicated with more tourists and scholars about American history than any other institution, surpassing even the entire collection of museums that comprise the Smithsonian Institution. We have discussed the NPS throughout this chapter but now we need to address how it substantially revamped its approach to discussing information and authenticity in recent years. We describe the size and scope of the NPS in shaping the public's view of history; then consider the range of visitors NPS deals with, by categorizing these individuals through an information lens. We conclude this account with a discussion of how the NPS responded to new historiography and to the public,

Table 5.2 Civil War Battlefield Parks Managed by the National Park Service (NPS)

Antietam National Battlefield
Battle of Chancellorsville
Battle of Fredericksburg
Brices Cross Roads National Battlefield Site
Chickamauga and Chattanooga National Military Park
Fort Donelson National Battlefield
Fort Sumter National Monument
Fredericksburg and Spotsylvania National Military Park
Gettysburg National Military Park
Kennesaw Mountain National Battlefield Park
Manassas National Battlefield
Monocacy National Battlefield
Pea Ridge National Military Park
Petersburg National Battlefield
Richmond National Battlefield Park
Shiloh National Military Park
Stones River National Battlefield
Tennessee Civil War Heritage Area
Vicksburg National Military Park
Wilson's Creek National Battlefield

in large part by reimagining a new museum and visitor's center. That last event allows us to begin re-integrating the five major issues influencing interpretations of the battle and the Civil War.

NPS manages all the key Civil War battlefields, also those of the American Revolution and other conflicts (e.g., the War of 1812, the Indian wars).[73] NPS also manages the millions of acres of national parks, such as Yellowstone. In 2020 alone—the last year before COVID caused a decline in visits—237 million Americans visited the more than 400 sites managed by the NPS.[74] Table 5.2 lists the numerous NPS sites connected with the Civil War—a preponderance of the places people visit to learn about and experience this war. The messages, policies, and practices for these multiple parks is centralized in the NPS headquarter offices within the US Department of the Interior in Washington, DC. In other words, programmatic decisions are national in scope, intended to be consistent across all its sites, with only minor variations allowed at individual localities, to account for the specifics of the historical events being explained.

NPS operates more than 160 historic sites pertaining to all periods of American history, and partially operates fifty-five "National Heritage Areas." NPS also administers fourteen military cemeteries, most of them located at battlefield sites, including Antietam, Fort Donelson, Fredericksburg, Gettysburg, Shiloh, Stones River, and Vicksburg. In short, NPS has communicated with more people, over a longer period of time, at the most important battle sites, than all other American institutions; and thus it has had the greatest influence on public perception of the authentic history of the Civil War.

NPS also holds massive collections of relevant military objects. All the battlefield parks preserve weapons and uniforms and have built up substantial libraries and collections of manuscripts, maps, and photographs for use by their staffs and other historians. One real challenge for NPS beyond preserving a site and its ephemera has been to compress details of what happened into a comprehensible whole while simultaneously dramatizing events to stimulate interest and to "sell" its desired impression. NPS management has faced this challenge since the 1930s, notably in Gettysburg because of its popularity as a heritage site.[75] As an NPS director in 1931 declared, "Historical activity is primarily not a research program but an educational program in the broader sense."[76]

Preservation was necessarily linked to the public interpretation of events. Gettysburg's history has been preserved and documented since the 1860s. A major change took place once the NPS took control in 1933. Its work over the years has been characterized by improved museum curation practices, professional research by historians, and communication with the public grounded increasingly in empirical research. This latter task has proved challenging because NPS had to figure out how to address raw, ugly truths (e.g., brutality of war, slavery as the cause of the Civil War) and reach multiple constituencies believing in the reconciliation myth. The park's management relied upon interpretations provided by specialists rather than by the public, local merchants, politicians, or veterans. The NPS track record is one of partial success. They have deviated in some respects from the highly sanitized—and hence inauthentic—interpretation of events. But this has created tension with the various interested parties, which has existed since the 1930s, varying in degree by site and by event.[77] At Gettysburg, the NPS had to reign in private guides as late as the 1960s, increasingly insisting on accuracy and conformity of message. (How reminiscent this is of Lotte Schoen's play-acting battles with Lettice Douffet that we described at the beginning of chapter 1.)

NPS's task was made more difficult by the shifting interests of historians. In Gettysburg, the shift was increasingly away from studying military tactics and strategies to concern for wider issues about how best to commemorate and remember not only the military events but also the related social and cultural issues. NPS has typically made good use of its greatest assets at Gettysburg Park: the land where the battle had actually occurred and the artifacts from the battle. Over time, how those assets were employed by NPS evolved as historical interests and historical understanding changed.[78]

We focus here on the debates surrounding authenticity in the form and content of the narrative at Gettysburg in the 1990s and early 2000s. Nothing focuses the attention of a park's administration more intensely than the decisions required when building a new museum because what messages it wants to communicate need to be reflected in how a building is configured, what artifacts are selected to exhibit, and how the narrative is constructed.

The first museum on the Gettysburg site had been built in the 1960s. It was crammed full of guns, bullets, bayonets, photographs, and letters; and it told the story of the military events and proclaimed the reconciliation message. The commemoration of the Civil War's centennial in 1963 attracted more than two million visitors to the park that year, reinforcing in the visitors' minds the NPS account of the battle. But not all tourists found the experience "accurate," or "authentic" (e.g., the reenactments in particular were regarded by some visitors as near-circus events). Over the next decade, management debated what to do regarding messaging and landscaping, while expanding their capability to handle the ever-increasing numbers of visitors. In the 1970s and 1980s, messaging focused upon who fought at Gettysburg, who stayed home, and Lincoln the man. Park rangers took tourists around to explain tactical battlefield issues on the actual battle sites. In the 1990s, movies about Gettysburg added to the public's interest and their perceived knowledge of events.

This original museum was regarded as part of a larger problem of authentic presentation of the war and the nation.[79] There were criticisms that the museum had a disorganized exhibit of thousands of artifacts. Historians perceived that the park lacked a cohesive narrative about either the battle at Gettysburg or the broader issues of the Civil War.

Management realized that the majority of visitors were White males, and the site needed to attract a broader audience. To achieve that goal called for new areas of focus, including discussions of the causes of the Civil War and a more encompassing story. The Civil Rights movement of the 1960s and 1970s, together with a new generation of social historians, were having an effect, too. Both the topics and the facts seen as being authentic were changing. Throughout the 1990s, the main constituencies weighed in with their complaints. White Southerners complained about Lost Cause perspectives being minimized; African Americans argued that slavery was being ignored. The staff wanted to expand their interpretation of events. A panel of distinguished historians encouraged the park to broaden its views as the NPS thought through the planning for what a new museum might look like, a project the NPS expected to implement in the late 1990s or early 2000s.

NPS management from around the country periodically met to discuss operational issues during the 1990s. In 2000, Congress directed the Secretary of the Interior, and we quote directly from the directive because it had the force of law, to "encourage Civil War battle sites to recognize and include in all of their public displays and multi-media educational presentations the unique role that the institution of slavery played in causing the Civil War and its role, if any, at the individual sites."[80] Park officials and historians gathered to discuss how to implement this Congressional mandate.

In 2008, the NPS opened its new Gettysburg Museum, at a cost more than $100 million. During the early 2000s, the park had erected new signage throughout the park, re-landscaped the site to make it look as it had in the 1860s, added period fencing, and dismantled buildings constructed in the decades after the battle. It added more programs and lectures.[81] Tours were filmed and made available online. Despite all this effort, the public was divided on the success of the museum, based mostly on one's personal perspective on authenticity.

From the NPS viewpoint, the American public still viewed the Civil War through a military lens, while Congress and the professional historians saw it as a wider event in American history. Americans deemed the presentation to be authentic if the narrative discussed the role of military participants; and they expected to see period ephemera, accurately landscaped battlefields, and accurate military accounts of events. Authenticity in this framework did not involve linking military events to other social, political, and economic realities of the 1860s. How to address that linking problem became one of the major challenges faced by the museum's builders.

In the end, reviews of the museum were generally positive. One reviewer celebrated the fact that the new museum and visitor center introduced a richer, more coherent "story line than any other Civil War museum," using a mix of media ranging from video to artifacts to letters by soldiers and civilians—all told in the context of a horrific event.[82] Another reviewer noted that visitors were now invited to ask new questions, such as "Why they [soldiers] gave their lives to both cause and comrades," and "was Lincoln correct when he said that 'these dead shall not have died in vain'?"[83] Visitors were now exposed to causes and consequences of the Civil War. The center began with the constitutional debates over slavery and the causes of the war, and eventually presented the details of what occurred at Gettysburg. Visitors confronted issues about diverging economic and social systems—slave economics versus an industrializing free labor society—setting up a power struggle that degenerated into a shooting war. The exhibits did not take sides, but instead presented issues as tensions and struggles that animated events of the 1850s and 1860s. The visitor was told that while the issue of preserving the union and the fate of slavery were resolved by the war, a third issue, the common rights and responsibilities of citizenship, remained unresolved. The exhibits avoided judgments about who was "right" or "wrong" in the war, shifting the debate away from issues NPS had similarly avoided in prior decades.

The building design projected a chronological narrative on visitors as they were introduced to slaves, women, soldiers, civilians, political events, emancipation, the home front, Lincoln's visit to the park, and other topics. Much of this information was used to provide context before presenting information about the battle itself. Along the way, myths were quietly dismantled, most notably those concerning Pickett's charge. This presentation avoided rhetoric of glory or nobility, and instead focused on the realities of bad strategy and tactics in the face of more modern killing technologies—and of the brutish outcome. Photographs of piles of dead soldiers forced the visitor to consider a new paradigm about authentic warfare. The exhibit forced the tourist to face their own, and the nation's, accountability for what happened. They could no longer think of history the way they were taught in school as a collection of chronologically placed facts. The truth was more complex, as we described above, in table 5.1. The NPS had realized its goal of making the visitor center a place of education, more than of entertainment or nostalgic sentimentality.

The visitors who came to Gettysburg had various profiles and expectations. They included the visitor unfamiliar with the battle and the war, the Civil War buffs keen about understanding the specific military events and the minutiae of Union armaments, university professors, military veterans, and descendants of those who had fought in the battle. That was true before and at the time of the new museum. However, in the past, NPS had also been charged with maintaining and instilling a patriotic (think nationalist) perspective as part of the nation's more than century-long definition of authenticity in battlefield presentations. Entertainment was also a part of the experience that had to be designed in to keep visitor numbers high. Each different visiting population measured its satisfaction with Gettysburg on its own personal interests and perspectives. This set up a contest between populations of visitors as to the true meaning of Gettysburg and the Civil War. The one clear trend in understanding Gettysburg, however, at the time of the new museum was the need to understand the Gettysburg's experience within a broader context of American history.[84]

Table 5.3 provides an overview of the various constituencies visiting Gettysburg in recent years. It was a considerable challenge for the park staff to get the messaging correct.[85] Civil War buffs are at times fanatical in their demand for precise, technical minutia. They might criticize a statue in the park for displaying an inauthentic hat worn by a soldier, or the wrong rifle in the 1860s photograph of a dead Confederate sharpshooter. The tourist might be someone who wants an ancestor's death at the battle vindicated. These visitors might have a preconceived notion of what happened and its implications, but they might not be as fanatical. The largest portion of visitors are simply individuals coming with their families, and their goal is both to get an education and be entertained; these tourists were generally accepting of what the tour guides told them.

The park's management knew from decades of working with visitors that to satisfy most visitor's desire for authenticity they had to provide an immersive experience, involving factual information, images, music, visits to the battlefield, seeing the weapons, and generally feeling what happened. It was a combination of offering the visitor an intellectual, emotional, and physical experience.[86] The park's staff had finally begun to shake off the near stranglehold of reconciliation narrative. They slowly reformed what constituted an authentic account by adding narratives about the causes and consequences of the war, while tamping down the earlier points of view.[87] They contended with what

Table 5.3   Types of Visitors to the Gettysburg Battlefield Park, circa 2015

Typical Museum Visitors	Who They Are	Their Expectations
Explorers	Curious and generally interested in what happened	Want a light overview of events and to see artifacts and fields. Recognize Gettysburg as important. Consider museums unquestionably authoritative. Park historians refer to original documents, hence accurate.
Facilitators	Want to satisfy desires of others that they care about	They want to relate to, e.g., what an ancestor might have experienced. Trust historians.
Experience seekers	Normally tourists there to enjoy an experience so they can feel like "they had been there"	Desire to learn what happened, walk the battlegrounds accurately displayed and factually not disturbing. Expect truth and question what does not comport to their expectations.
Professionals/ hobbyists	Smallest cohort such as historians and Civil War buffs; normally most influential in messaging	Intensely specific in wanting to know facts, reaffirm their own interpretations, and to engage or challenge experts. Trust the truth of facts.
Rechargers	Desire to bask in the wonder of the park	Often people who visit the park multiple times to reflect, rejuvenate, or enjoy the experience.

Source: Framework based on John H. Falk, *Identity and the Museum Visitor Experience* (Walnut Creek, CA: Left Coast Press, 2009), 190–203.

Athinodoros Chronis called "an imaginary zone," not simply a "physical spot," and for Southerners a "landscape of regret."[88] The sesquicentennial of the Civil War in 2013 brought heightened attention to military parks and an increase in visitors. It became clear that new story lines needed to be added, for example to attract African Americans to the museum. Keeping Gettysburg relevant for changing audiences was and is fundamentally a discussion about authenticity. Historian Peter Carmichael acknowledged as much, arguing that the challenge ahead was keeping battlefields relevant "without losing the emotional resonance that people crave from historic sites."[89]

IMPLICATIONS FOR UNDERSTANDING GETTYSBURG AND AUTHENTICITY

A case study of Gettysburg has much to teach us about authenticity. The large numbers of visitors over a century and a half provides us, in the language of social scientists, more data points than the smaller heritage sites of Lindsborg and Williamsburg. Our discussions of what insights smaller heritage sites provided regarding authenticity could thus be further tested against the Gettysburg experience. Given that visitors brought a variety of perspectives, agendas, and expectations with them to visit Gettysburg, the story is complex.

Visitors to Gettysburg have always expected that a narrative with a point of view was going to be presented. In fact, the many different types of people with an interest in Gettysburg demanded it, including the various visitor groups: local merchants and citizens, politicians, the US Congress, the military, veterans, school children, West Point cadets, academic historians, Civil War buffs, families on a day-long adventure, career military, Southerners, Northerners, and veterans of this battle. This narrative had to have meaning, even if that meaning evolved over time. The American public has long embraced moral lessons, and so it was with Gettysburg: morality and religious teachings shaped and continue to shape the "lessons of history" from this battlefield. All of this had to be done, too, within the constraints of technically correct military history because the visitors noticed actual and perceived errors in the presentation.[90]

Within months after the battle, the site and its history were swept up into the larger questions about the Civil War—and increasingly since the 1980s into the even larger questions about race in American society. Lindsborg addressed one small piece of the important issue of immigration for Americans and Williamsburg addressed some issues of race and gender, but both paled beside Gettysburg's direct struggle with Civil War and race.

In all periods, we find that Americans wanted historical authenticity, even if they could not agree on what that meant. Museums seemed to be the only widely accepted, neutral territory where all constituencies would at least grudgingly acknowledge authenticity exists. They had in their favor objects representing historical accuracy—artifacts and documentation (letters, photographs) with a well-established provenance, cared for and interpreted by trained experts. Even so, visitors to an historic site can be skeptical about the specifics of a particular artifact or questioning about whether the park historians are too pro-Union (for history, many believed, is written by the victors).[91] As observed with Williamsburg, what constituted "real history" is contested, although tourists at Gettysburg seemed to respect the accounts of the better-trained, uniformed federal park rangers, perhaps more than tour guides garbed in period costumes at Williamsburg. (Williamsburg had several hundred trained experts, such as historians, conservators, and archivists, but Gettysburg had access to many more through the combination of experts on site and in the park headquarters in Washington, DC, and at other facilities.) But as at Williamsburg, their credibility was always subject to criticism if, for example, the property was too clean, the fences too recently repainted, the grounds not reflective of what the landscape looked like in 1863, or a docent wore sneakers. A Vietnam or World War II veteran would expect to see more mud than grass and wonder why trees did not have broken branches.

Gettysburg's experience teaches us not to blame "ignorant tourists" because they are voters who can outmaneuver the NPS through their Congressional delegations. Heritage sites and national parks have to earn the respect of their visitors. The average tourist is perhaps less likely to identify with Williamsburg or Lindsborg, more so with Gettysburg and other battlefield parks. Many of these visitors had ancestors who fought, died, or were wounded in the Civil War; and for them, these sites were personal. Museums and the sites themselves thus become channels for engaging with the authenticity of a national event, and never more so than with a civil war.

One can be impressed with yet another feature of authenticity: its ability to remain relatively constant while being simultaneously transforming. This seems counterintuitive. For example, reconciliation existed as a theme for more than 150 years, even as the historical reputations of major figures from the Gettysburg battlefield, such as Robert E. Lee, radically changed over time.[92] Myths endure, despite facts. Thirteen hundred monuments became stone and metal redoubts reinforcing myths.

We have discussed constructivism as a central theme as we discussed that authenticity is a concept in motion. Recall, constructivism is the idea that people create—construct and shape—information or perceived knowledge of a subject rather than accept passively someone else's interpretation of facts. This dynamic is always front and center at Gettysburg. Thousands of books about the battle, and the more than 130 million visitors indicate the ongoing constructivist guerrilla war at Gettysburg.[93] Constructivism reshapes the narrative of what happened and why. That is why what is presented is never perfect, or absolute in its truth, underlying what shapes and makes possible the evolution of authenticity. The public does not always demand absolutes, but instead general conformance to its expectations of what constitutes accurate experiences and facts. A park ranger encountering what many of them would call the "Civil War crazies" with their strong views about the war, can sometimes wonder about the relativism of these truths.

One lesson to be derived from Gettysburg is that its guardians since the 1930s have strived to be as intellectually empirical as was possible. They typically worked apart from the private museums surrounding their park, such as the historic homes in Gettysburg, which did not always provide as rigorously researched history as NPS demanded. Ghost stories are widespread about Gettysburg, but they are not told by park rangers on federal property. Two anthropologists may have captured the essence of the continuing evolution of authenticity at heritage sites when they argued that people behave in "divided consciousness." By that they mean people "continue to be preoccupied with the past as the last refuge of the really real" but at the same time "some of them, at least, allow for the possibility that the really real is myth."[94]

Myths are part of the story. We mentioned earlier a West point historian, General Seidule, raised on Lost Cause mythology in Virginia, taking decades to overcome it. More than just a Southerner, he was a trained military historian, a career Army officer, an expert on the warfare of the Civil War, and a graduate of Washington and Lee University (where Robert E. Lee is buried and which is a shrine to his Lost Cause mythology). He lamented at the end of his 2020 book that the memory of the Civil War "remains contested." He called for acknowledging facts, "not myth and not ideology."[95]

Historians and park guides at Gettysburg relied on one weapon to counter mythologies, to understand the nature of expected authenticity, and to explain what happened, what was called "credibility armor" when describing how staff at Williamsburg went about shaping their messages to the public and guiding their restoration work. Leaders in Lindsborg did not don such credibility armor, instead relying more on impressions, mythology, and tourist expectations of what constituted authenticity. The Gettysburg experience demonstrates that such loose standards for truth were not tolerated as much by tourists at national heritage sites. Coming to Lindsborg or Williamsburg was less of a serious excursion than walking through a battlefield or a military cemetery attached to it. The mood at Gettysburg is less celebratory than at Williamsburg—this is palpable to anyone who has visited both sites.

This concludes our third and largest case study. In the final chapter, we compare the three case studies of Lindsborg, Williamsburg, and Gettysburg. We use some of the theorizing from our first two chapters to understand better the lessons one can draw from these three heritage sites. Finally, we draw some conclusions for tourism scholars, information scholars, and the general reader.

NOTES

1. Guest columnist, "Letter to the Editor: Remove Confederate Statues on the Gettysburg Battlefield," *Evening Sun*, June 24, 2020, https://www.evening-sun.com/story/opinion/2020/06/24/confederate-statues-remove-letter-to-the-editor-gettysburg/3250680001/.

2. The specific military units that were involved were identified in the subsequent two decades and so not the subject of much controversy.

3. National Park Service, statistics for 1934 through 2020, https://irma.nps.gov/STATS/SSRSReports/Park%20Specific%20Reports/Annua%2020Park%20Recreation%20Visitation%20(1904%20-%20Last%20Calendar%20Year)?Park=GETT(accessed January 30, 2022).

4. This landmass does not include many additional thousands of surrounding acreage one could argue is part of the historic locality of military action and deployment.

5. National Park Service, "Collections," https://www.nps.gov/gett/learn/historyculture/collections.htm (accessed January 30, 2022).

6. One scholar estimates more than thirty thousand books about the battle at Gettysburg. (Jonathan Sarna, "Review: *The Jewish Confederates*," *American Jewish History* 89, no. 3 [2001]: 335–37.)

7. These statistics do not include scholarly and general trade articles, nor to the hundreds of websites devoted to the subject.

8. Jennifer M. Murray, "'Far Above Our Poor Power to Add or Detract': National Park Service Administration of the Gettysburg Battlefield, 1933–1938," *Civil War History* 55, no. 1 (2009): 56.

9. For useful accounts, among many of the speech, Kent Gramm, *Lincoln's Elegy at Gettysburg* (Bloomington: Indiana University Press, 2001); Martin Johnson, *Writing the Gettysburg Address* (Lawrence: University of Kansas Press, 2013).

10. Thomas A. Desjardin, *These Honored Dead: How the Story of Gettysburg Shaped American History* (Cambridge MA: De Capo Press, 2003): first quote xv, second quote xvi.

11. The issue of proper landscaping has been such a contested issue over the decades that a historiography has developed about it rooted in discussions about the nature of authenticity. Key studies include, Brian Black, *Gettysburg Contested: 150 Years of Preserving America's Cherished Landscape* (Staunton, VA: George F. Thompson Publishing, 2019) and his earlier "The Nature of Preservation: The Rise of Authenticity at Gettysburg," *Civil War History* 58, no. 3 (September 2012): 348–73.

12. Michelle Singletary and Spencer S. Hsu, "Disney Says VA. Park Will Be Serious Fun," *Washington Post*, November 12, 1993, https://www.washington-post.com/archive/politics/1993/11/12/disney-says-va-park-will-be-serious-fun/a1c0ef16-ae33-4d99-a489-3fbfeedd1c7b/ (accessed January 31, 2022); Richard Perez-Pena, "Disney Drops Plan for History Theme Park in Virginia," *New York Times*, September 29, 1994, https://www.nytimes.com/1994/09/29/us/disney-drops-plan-for-history-theme-park-in-virginia.html (accessed January 31, 2022); Michael Kelleher, "Images of the Past: Historical Authenticity and Inauthenticity from Disney to Times Square," *CRM Journal* (Summer 2004): 6–19. The people at Colonial Williamsburg were similarly concerned about the effects of this proposed theme park.

13. Desjardin, *These Honored Dead*, 6–7.

14. Amy J. Kinsel, "From Turning Point to Peace Memorial: A Cultural Legacy," in *The Gettysburg Nobody Knows*, edited by Gabor Boritt, 203–22 (New York: Oxford University Press, 1997).

15. For a history of this battle of truths versus contested memories, see J. Christian Spielvogel, *Interpreting Sacred Ground: The Rhetoric of National Civil War Parks and Battlefields* (Tuscaloosa: University of Alabama Press, 2013); Amy J. Kinsel, "'From These Honored Dead': Gettysburg in American Culture, 1863–1938" (unpublished PhD diss., Cornell University, 1992); Edward Tabor Linenthal, *Sacred Ground: Americans and Their Battlefields* (Urbana: University of Illinois Press, 1991); further on the role of memory, Jim Weeks, *Gettysburg: Memory, Market, and an American Shrine* (Princeton, NJ: Princeton University Press, 2003), Carol Reardon, *Pickett's Charge in History and Memory* (Chapel Hill: University of North Caroline Press, 1997), and by one of the most distinguished historians of the Civil War, David Blight, *Race and Reunion: The Civil War in American Memory* (Cambridge, MA: Harvard University Press, 2001).

16. While many heritage sites refer to tourists as *tourists* or *customers*, the word *visitor* is more frequently invoked when discussing those who came to a national, often battlefield park. The word is recognition that not everyone comes for pleasure, rather to venerate and to learn about a serious, somewhat sad, yet important event touching their lives. It is not uncommon for men to

take their hats off when walking through a military cemetery, Gettysburg's too, and for visitors to speak in hushed tones in the cemetery and to contemplate in silence the events from the spot where soldiers made Pickett's Charge that cost the Confederacy some six thousand lives in thirty minutes on July 3, 1863, or similarly at Little Round Top and other spots in the park.

17. Athinodoros Chronis and Ronald D. Hampton, "Consuming the Authentic Gettysburg: How a Tourist Landscape Becomes an Authentic Experience," *Journal of Consumer Behavior* 7 (2008): 119.

18. Locational accuracy in the monuments was often somewhat compromised because of NPS policy regarding where monuments could be placed. NPS established a rule that said a regimental monument had to be placed at the spot where a military unit was at the moment it entered an engagement (known as the "line of battle" rule which required monuments to be placed where troops "entered the fight"). In the case of the Confederates, who initiated the majority of the fights (think charges) that meant placing monuments as much as a mile away from whatever event they are remembered for, not where their action occurred. Pickett's charge is an example. This reality is even before one discusses the accuracy of the text on those monuments, Desjardin, *These Honored Dead*, 156–57.

19. On the movies and an analysis of Ken Burns' PBS series, see Desjardin, *These Honored Dead*, 144–52, 177–91.

20. Spielvogel, *Interpreting Sacred Ground*, 152; see the parks' website for details, https://www.nps.gov/gett/learn/index.htm; Barry Mackintosh, "The National Park Services Moves into Historical Interpretation," *The Public Historian* 9, no. 2 (1987): 50–63; and the most detailed source, Jennifer Marie Murray, "'On a Great Battlefield': The Making, Management, and Memory of Gettysburg National Military Park, 1933–2009" (unpublished PhD diss., Auburn University, 2010).

21. National Park Service news release, "Tourism to Gettysburg and Eisenhower Parks Creates $92 Million Economic Benefits," April 27, 2018, https://www.nps.gov/gett/learn/news/tourism-benefits-2017.htm (accessed January 31, 2022).

22. J. A. Costa and G. J. Bammossy, "Le Parc Disney: Creating an Authentic American Experience," in *Advances in Consumer Research*, edited by M. C. Gilly and J. Meyers-Levy, 398–402 (Valdosta, GA: Association for Consumer Research, 2001); Chronis and Hampton, "Consuming the Authentic Gettysburg," 122–23.

23. Rory Turner, "Bloodless Battles: The Civil Ware Reenacted," *TDR* 34, no. 4 (winter 1990): 123–36; Christopher Bates, "Civil Rights Meets the Civil War Centennial: The 100th Anniversary Reenactments of Manassas and Gettysburg," *UCLA Historical Journal* 21 (2006), https://escholarship.org/content/qt4jc0v1rp/qt4jc0v1rp.pdf (accessed February 1, 2022); Athinodoros Chronis,

"Between Place and Story: Gettysburg as Tourism Imaginary," *Annals of Tourism Research* 39, no. 4 (October 2012): 1797–816.

24. Gabor S. Boritt, *The Gettysburg Nobody Knows* (New York: Oxford University Press, 1997); Desjardin, *These Honored Dead*, see also his excellent bibliography, 227–32; Mark Grimsley and Brooks D. Simpson, *Gettysburg: A Battlefield Guide* (Lincoln: University of Nebraska Press, 1999); James M. McPherson, *Hallowed Ground: A Walk at Gettysburg* (New York: Crown Publishers, 2003).

25. While the volume of published discussion of these is vast, for useful summaries of the debates, see Desjardin, *These Honored Dead.*

26. See, for example, John W. Busey and David G. Martin, *Regimental Strengths and Losses at Gettysburg*, fourth edition (Hightstown, NJ: Longstreet House, 2005): 125, 260; Joseph T. Glatther, *General Lee's Army: From Victory to Collapse* (New York: Free Press, 2008): 282; Stephen W. Sears, *Gettysburg* (Boston, MA: Houghton Mifflin, 2003). We say "so far" because it is not unusual for any battlefield park to uncover remains of soldiers; it happens at most battlefields anywhere and from every century. When that happens in the United States, the US Army takes charge to identify the soldier (regardless of when he died), to provide a formal military funeral with the same rituals as if he had died last week, and military cemeteries provide a resting spot and gravestone, even if it has to be marked "Unknown." Tourists are welcomed to observe such events, but without a park promoting them.

27. Nearly every account of the battle by professional historians participated in the debate about significance. See for one example, Spielvogel, *Interpreting Sacred Ground.*

28. Joseph J. Cook, "'Of the People, by the People, for the People': The Transformation of Gettysburg Battlefield Park from a Site of Official Culture to a Popular Tourist Attraction," *Saber and Scroll Journal* 5, no. 2 (September 2016): 88. For two widely respected discussions of the evolution of the Park's significance, James M. McPherson, *What They Fought For, 1861–1865* (New York: Random House, 1995); Robert Penn Warren, *The Legacy of the Civil War* (Lincoln: University of Nebraska Press, 1998).

29. On Gettysburg as a turning point or "high water mark" of the Confederacy, Desjardin, *These Honored Dead*, 94–107, the quote, 94.

30. It would take us too far afield to bibliographically trace the histories of these individual myths.

31. Desjardin, *These Honored Dead*, 83–107.

32. Quoted in Desjardin, *These Honored Dead*, 88–89.

33. See Leon Reed, *Stories the Monuments Tell: A Photo Tour of Gettysburg, Told by Its Monuments* (Gettysburg, PA: Little Falls Press, n.d.): unpaginated. For a history of the monuments and their messages, see Desjardin, *These Honored Dead*, 153–76. On Confederate memorialization, see Edward T. O'Connell, "Public Commemoration of the Civil War and Monuments to Memory: The

Triumph of Robert E. Lee and the Lost Cause" (unpublished PhD diss., Stony Brook University, 2008).

34. O'Connell, "Public Commemoration of the Civil War and Monuments to Memory," 51.

35. O'Connell, "Public Commemoration of the Civil War and Monuments to Memory," 51.

36. Murray, "On a Great Battlefield," 44.

37. Murray, "On a Great Battlefield," 3.

38. Desjardin, *These Honored Dead*, 176.

39. Desjardin, *These Honored Dead*, 65.

40. The role of violence in the battle at Gettysburg, for example, is getting attention, Jack Pittenger, "'A Good Place to Focus on the Human Cost and Agony': The Interpretation of Violence and Trauma at Gettysburg National Military Park" (unpublished PhD diss., Arizona State University, 2013); Spielvogel, *Interpreting Sacred Ground*. Other issues involve the role of reconciliation as a device to settle the contested presidential election of 1876 and closure of Reconstruction that made possible the ex-Confederate states to create the Jim Crow regime.

41. The 1938 event was shown in the last episode of Ken Burns' PBS nine-part series, *The Civil War*. Some 25 veterans of the battle were present at this last reunion, most participating in the restaging of the handshake, while over 2000 other Civil War veterans looked on.

42. It ceased to exist in 1956 with the death of its last surviving member.

43. O'Connell, "Public Commemoration of the Civil War and Monuments to Memory," 62–118.

44. O'Connell, "Public Commemoration of the Civil War and Monuments to Memory," 110. On the history of reconciliation see, David W. Blight, *Race and Reunion: The Civil War in American Memory* (Cambridge, MA: Belknap Press of Harvard University Press, 2001); Desjardin, *These Honored Dead*.

45. O'Connell, "Public Commemoration of the Civil War and Monuments to Memory," first quote 118, second quote 122.

46. O'Connell, "Public Commemoration of the Civil War and Monuments to Memory," 126.

47. Thomas Lawrence Connelly, *The Marble Man: Robert E. Lee and His Image in American Society* (Baton Rouge: Louisiana State University Press, 1978); Gaines M. Foster, *Ghosts of the Confederacy: Defeat, the Lost Cause, and the Emergence of the New South, 1865 to 1913* (New York: Oxford University Press, 1987); William Garrett Piston, *Lee's Tarnished Lieutenant: James Longstreet and His Place in Southern History* (Athens: University of Georgia Press, 1987); Gary W. Gallagher and Alan T. Nolan, *The Myth of the Lost Cause and Civil War History* (Bloomington: Indiana University Press, 2000); Paul M. Gaston, *The New South Creed: A Study in Southern Myth-Making* (New York: Vintage

Books, 1973); Edward Alfred Pollard, *The Lost Cause; A New Southern History of the War of the Confederates* (Los Angeles, CA: HardPress, 2018).

48. Rollin G. Osterweis, *The Myth of the Lost Cause, 1865–1900* (Hamden, CT: Archon Books, 1973), ix.

49. Gallagher and Nolan, *The Myth of the Lost Cause and Civil War History*, 13–14; Robert Taylor, *Cavalier and Yankee: The Old South and American Character* (Cambridge, MA: Harvard University Press, 1979); Blight, *Race and Reunion*, 255–99.

50. O'Connell, "Public Commemoration of the Civil War and Monuments to Memory," 156.

51. O'Connell, "Public Commemoration of the Civil War and Monuments to Memory," 156.

52. O'Connell, "Public Commemoration of the Civil War and Monuments to Memory," 175.

53. For a brilliant assessment of the Lost Cause thesis and the memory of the Civil War, see a lecture by David Blight, "Legacies of the Civil War," YouTube, November 21, 2008, https://www.youtube.com/watch?v=yesO9SnEQ6Y (accessed February 3, 2022).

54. Zack Stanton, "How Trumpism Is Becoming America's New 'Lost Cause,'" *Politico*, January 21, 2021, http://www.davidwblight.com/public-history/2021/1/22/how-trumpism-is-becoming-americas-new-lost-cause-politico (accessed February 3, 2022); Desjardin, *These Honored Dead*, 125.

55. Gerald F. Linderman, *Embattled Courage: The Experiences of Combat in the American Civil War* (New York: Free Press, 1987), 267.

56. Reid Mitchell, *Civil War Soldiers* (New York: Penguin, 1988); Jonathan Shay, *Achilles in Vietnam: Combat Trauma and the Undoing of Character* (New York: Atheneum, 1994).

57. Brent Nosworthy, *The Bloody Crucible of Courage: Fighting Methods and Combat Experience of the Civil War* (New York: Carroll and Graf Publishers, 2003). For a review of the violence historiography, see Pittenger, "'A Good Place to Focus on the Human Cost and Agony,'" 1–32.

58. Pittenger, "'A Good Place to Focus on the Human Cost and Agony,'" 22.

59. Pittenger, "'A Good Place to Focus on the Human Cost and Agony,'" 65.

60. Nikole Hannah-Jones, Caitlin Roper, Ilena Silverman, and Jake Silverstein (eds.), *The 1619 Project: A New Origin Story* (New York: One World, 2021).

61. While Blacks did not fight in Gettysburg, they did fight on the Union side in other battles in the Civil War.

62. Brian Matthew Jordan, "'We Stand on the Same Battlefield': The Gettysburg Centenary and the Shadow of Race," *The Pennsylvania Magazine of History and Biography* 135, no. 4 (October 2011): 481–511.

63. Blight, *Race and Reunion*, 3.

64. "Black Soldiers in the US Military During the Civil War," National Archives, https://www.archives.gov/education/lessons/blacks-civil-war (accessed February 3, 2022).

65. Rachel Nicholas, "African Americans During the Gettysburg Campaign," National Park Service: Gettysburg, June 1, 2020, https://www.nps.gov/gett/blogs/african-americans-during-the-gettysburg-campaign.htm (accessed February 3, 2022).

66. For details of the Confederate Army's rounding up of African Americans during Lee's invasion, see Ty Seidule, *Robert E. Lee and Me: A Southerner's Reckoning with Myth of the Lost Cause* (New York: St. Martin's Press, 2020), 232–33. The author is a retired US Army general and historian who taught Civil War military history at West Point. This book is the most thorough indictment of the mythology surrounding Lee available written by a professional historian. Contrast this account with that of NPS's own Gettysburg historian, Thomas A. Desjardin, who explained his employer's gentle move toward dismantling that part of Civil War mythology surrounding slavery, concerned not to overly confront expectations of tourists and other visitors concerning what they thought was authentic.

67. Nikole Hannah-Jones, "Justice," in Hannah-Jones, Roper, Silverman, and Silverstein, *The 1619 Project*, 452.

68. Blight, *Race and Reunion*, 2.

69. Blight, *Race and Reunion*, 3.

70. James P. Weeks, "A Different View of Gettysburg: Play, Memory, and Race at the Civil War's Greatest Shrine," *Civil War History* 50, no. 2 (2004): 175–91; Lance R. Eisenhower, "'At Least Until We Shall Have an American Celebration to Take Its Place': African American Celebratory Excursions to Gettysburg, 1880–1915," *Donald T. Campbell Social Science Research Prize* (2017), http://preserve.lehigh.edu/cas-campbell-prize/41 (accessed February 4, 2022).

71. Weeks, "A Different View of Gettysburg: Play, Memory, and Race at the Civil War's Greatest Shrine," first quote 184, second quote 189.

72. Weeks, "A Different View of Gettysburg: Play, Memory, and Race at the Civil War's Greatest Shrine," 190–91.

73. NPS manages additional military parks related to other US wars. Sixty-one historic sites are designated as "National Historical Parks," another seventy-four are "National Historic Sites," nine as "National Military Parks" (e.g., Gettysburg), eleven as "National Battlefields," thirty-six as "national Memorials" (e.g., Vietnam and Lincoln Memorials). Differences in titles and designations do not indicate differentiation in how the parks are operated. They are all treated administratively equal.

74. NPS data, https://www.nps.gov/aboutus/visitation-numbers.htm (accessed February 5, 2022). The largest number of visitors to a single Smithsonian Museum in 2020 was to the American Art Museum (387,403), and to

the most visited museum, the National Museum of African American History and Culture (367,727) with all Smithsonian totals coming to 3.3 million, Smithsonian data, https://www.si.edu/newsdesk/about/stats (accessed February 5, 2022).

75. Mackintosh, "The National Park Service Moves into Historical Interpretation," 50–63.

76. Quoted in Mackintosh, "The National Park Service Moves into Historical Interpretation," 53.

77. For examples in range of authenticity at sites, Mackintosh, "The National Park Service Moves into Historical Interpretation," 56–57.

78. For a short history of the early years, Jennifer M. Murray, "'Far Above Our Poor Power to Add or Detract': National Park Service Administration of the Gettysburg Battlefield, 1933–1938," *Civil War History* 55, no. 1 (2009): 56–81; and her "'On A Great Battlefield': The Making, Management, and Memory of Gettysburg National Military Park, 1933–2009" (unpublished PhD diss., Auburn University, 2010).

79. Murray, "'Far Above Our Poor Power to Add or Detract,'" 430–37.

80. Quoted in Murray, "'On A Great Battlefield,'" 435.

81. Judith Giesberg, "The Museum and Visitor Center at Gettysburg National Military Park," *Pennsylvania History: A Journal of Mid-Atlantic Studies* 76, no. 3 (Summer 2009): 346–50.

82. Peter S. Carmichael, "The Gettysburg Museum of the American Civil War, Gettysburg, PA," *The Journal of American History* 96, no. 3 (December 2009): 804.

83. Carmichael, "The Gettysburg Museum of the American Civil War, Gettysburg, PA," 804.

84. James J. Broomall, Peter S. Carmichael, and Jill Ogline Titus, "The Future of Civil War History," *Civil War History* 62, no. 2 (June 2016): 120–30.

85. For an excellent discussion of the park, museum, and its messaging, see Ava M. Muhr, "Business, Education, and Enjoyment: Stakeholder Interpretations of the Gettysburg Museum and Visitors Center," *The Cupola: Scholarship at Gettysburg College* (spring 2015), https://cupola.gettysburg.edu/student_scholarship/313/ (accessed February 5, 2022).

86. For survey work on what visitors expected and experienced, Gatewood and Cameron, "Battlefield Pilgrims at Gettysburg National Military Park," 193–216.

87. Broomall, Carmichael, and Titus, "The Future of Civil War History," 124.

88. Athinodoros Chronis, "Between Place and Story: Gettysburg as Tourism Imaginary," *Annals of Tourism Research* 39, no. 4 (October 2012): 1798.

89. Chronis, "Between Place and Story," 129.

90. For an example of the specificity required and consequences when not perfect, see Bradley J. Klustner, "Interpreting a Commemorative Landscape:

The Eleventh Corps and Cemetery Hill," *The Cupola* (spring 2017) http://cupid
.gettysburg.edu/student_scholarship/519 (accessed February 6, 2022), which
deals with the actions of one military unit at one site on one day of the battle.

91. This aphorism has been attributed to both Winston Churchill and Hermann Goering, but in fact it probably was first stated much earlier. See Mathew
Phelan, "The History of 'History is Written by the Victors,'" *Slate*, November
26, 2019, https://slate.com/culture/2019/11/history-is-written-by-the-victors
-quote-origin.html (accessed March 24, 2022). Thus, another example of
misinformation!

92. For example, on the one hand, there was a widespread belief about the
saintly virtues of Robert E. Lee, but on the other hand he was a slave owner
who ran forced labor camps (his plantations), resigned from the US Army even
though he had taken an oath as an officer to defend the United States each time
he was promoted, and as a rebel general directly caused well over a hundred
thousand US soldiers to be killed, and in total loss of life in excess of 650,000
not to mention the 1.2 million people who suffered from battle wounds, disease, and other military-related accidents, or of being largely responsible for
the war continuing for an additional two years.

93. Eric Gable and Richard Handler, "After Authenticity at an American
Heritage Site," *American Anthropologist* 98, no. 2 (1996): 568–78. This article
focuses largely on Williamsburg as its specific case study, but can be general-
ized to discuss all American heritage sites.

94. Gable and Handler, "After Authenticity at an American Heritage Site,"
576.

95. Seidule, *Robert E. Lee and Me*, 255.

6

LESSONS ABOUT AUTHENTICITY AND MISINFORMATION

In this final chapter, we pull together findings about authenticity, misinformation, and how they relate to one another from our three case studies and our reviews of the scholarly literature in tourism studies and information studies. Tourism studies is a younger but more rapidly growing field compared to information studies, and we firmly believe that each of these disciplines can learn from the other. In this book, we have examined the authenticity-misinformation issue, but we are planning to examine other aspects of the tourism studies-information studies connections in future work. We have noted in earlier chapters the impact that tourists—hundreds of millions of them—have had on the themes we have explored. Now, with the pandemic appearing to diminish worldwide, many hundreds of millions of these tourists may be on the road again.

LESSONS FROM OUR THREE CASE STUDIES

Let us begin with some comparison of the three case studies. They focus on different periods of time and different issues. Colonial Williamsburg is about the eighteenth century and Lindsborg mainly focuses on the late nineteenth and early twentieth centuries, while Gettysburg falls in between, covering events primarily from the 1860s. All three heritage sites cover issues that are important to American history and to the American psyche. Lindsborg is mostly about immigration and ethnicity issues, and about local development. Williamsburg is mostly about everyday life in colonial America and lessons from this era about freedom, liberty, and patriotism; and it is secondarily about race. Gettysburg is about war tearing apart the nation, as well as about slavery and race.

It is clear from these studies that Gettysburg generally receives the most visceral response from visitors, Williamsburg next, and Lindsborg a distance third. This in part explains the differences between the three sites in the number of visitors. Lindsborg is swamped by a few thousand visitors on its important festival days but it has many fewer visitors at other times. The attendance at the other two sites has been much greater. Williamsburg had just over a million visitors in its busiest year, while Gettysburg has a million visitors almost every year. In recent years, attendance at Gettysburg has been approximately 1.6 times that at Williamsburg. Colonial Williamsburg has a healthy marketing budget to attract visitors. Gettysburg does not need to market heavily to have healthy attendance, although it does some marketing to diversity its audience. There seems to be a much larger population that feels a personal connection to the Civil War than to colonial times, the Revolutionary War, or European immigration.

Of the three cases, Gettysburg has a much longer, sustained history as a heritage site. While Williamsburg starts up in the late 1920s and Lindsborg's activities primarily get underway after the Second World War, Gettysburg has been of interest to the American public continuously since the 1860s. These cases also differ in their management histories. Gettysburg has had three successive managing organizations (volunteer veterans' organizations, the War Department, and the National Park Service), with somewhat different goals from one another; while Lindsborg and Williamsburg have had a single managing structure over time. One might say that Lindsborg follows a local development model, while Williamsburg follows a corporatist model and Gettysburg follows a national model.

In the cases of Lindsborg and Williamsburg, the people responsible for managing the heritage site had that site as their sole organizational responsibility. However, the National Park Service staff had responsibility not only for Gettysburg, but also for a number of other sites across the nation where historic events occurred or which are places of extraordinary natural beauty. NPS is public rather than private. These organizational characteristics had several implications for Gettysburg.

As a government agency, NPS staff were beholden to the nation in a way that neither Lindsborg nor Williamsburg were. This meant they were subject to the political whims of Congress. This led Gettysburg to a hybrid management system, with some rules set at the national headquarters in Washington, DC, but with enough flexibility to provide some local control to each of its many sites. For example, local staff in Gettysburg does the heavy lifting on messaging and digging up the specifics, for example, research, writing, preparing training guides, local regulation creation and enforcement, and dealing with multiple types of inquiry and behavior from visitors. This hybrid arrangement has led to both more skilled and extensive management, and more budgetary flexibility to carry out quality programming.

These case studies make clear the plasticity of information. Both creators and visitors at these sites change in their interests and backgrounds over time, and with these changes come not only changes in the factual information that is emphasized but also reexamination of what is factual. There are many stakeholders in the case of each of these heritage sites, and the sites can be regarded as information ecosystems. For example, the ecosystem in Lindsborg includes local merchants, residents, and business leaders interacting regularly over a long period of time over what messages and facts to emphasize. At Gettysburg, there is the NPS, local park staff, tourists, historians, local tourist trade merchants (e.g., motels, gift shops), and in earlier times, Civil War veterans. Thinking in terms of information ecosystems has assisted scholars in tracking the various stakeholders and how they interact.

Lindsborg has not been especially touched by changing historical interests; it has always been about cultural history and has had a single message to convey across time. Colonial Williamsburg has had one major change in messaging that came in during the 1960s and 1970s with the emergence of the new social history. For its early history, Williamsburg had only one primary message to convey—teaching American patriotic principles through the stories of the Revolutionary leaders. When the messaging changed in the 1960s and 1970s, it was mainly an issue of telling multiple stories, but these stories did not generally contradict one another. By contrast, from the very beginning, Gettysburg has had stakeholders interested in learning about messages that competed and contradicted one another. It was not nearly as simple as telling the multiple stories of the wealthy landowner, the tradesman, and the slaves that needed to occur in recent years at Williamsburg.

In the two larger case studies, of Williamsburg and Gettysburg, the immersive experience was particularly important to visitor satisfaction and a feeling of authenticity. It mattered that they were positioned at the actual site where these momentous events happened, restored as much as possible to the way they were at the time, using authentic artifacts (whether original or carefully reproduced) and historically accurate narratives to educate and entertain. For Lindsborg, there was not as much concern about making artifacts or narratives that were faithful to what happened in the home country of Sweden or even to early immigrant Lindsborg—it was more about creating an image of Swedishness than expressing the reality in great historical accuracy.

Motives were important, too. Lindsborg involvement in heritage activities was primarily driven by local economic development. While local businesses in Williamsburg and Gettysburg were also concerned about local economic development, Colonial Williamsburg was more concerned about protecting the message that attracted wealthy donors such as the Rockefellers and the Wallaces, and to provide an experience that was strong on both education and entertainment. Gettysburg has several different stakeholders with competing goals, ranging from those interested in the minutia of military details, to a place that honored veterans and their families and friends who had fought there, to an interpretation that gave both Southerners and Northerners a narrative that would make them feel good, to historians who wanted to understand the greater social and political context of Gettysburg in American history. Authenticity considerations at these heritage sites were often shaped by these various motives; everyone had an agenda.

We now turn to lessons learned from our first case study—of Lindsborg, Kansas. The process of turning Lindsborg into a public heritage site, which began in the 1960s, involved a process that turned private ritual into public ritual. Swedish culture that had taken place only privately in the home or semi-privately in the local church or social club was put on public display, for example in holiday celebrations intended for outside visitors. New signs of Swedish heritage, most notably the *Dala* horses, were added to public spaces. Swedish-themed gifts were sold in town to meet the local economic goals behind these celebrations targeted at visitors. To the degree there was any studious effort to study and preserve Swedish culture or Swedish-American culture, it took place through the local college (Bethany) and the museum/cultural center. However, expert knowledge did not prevail, and many citizens who participated in the Lindsborg ethnic festivals spoke up about what they believed was authentic. The goal in Lindsborg was much more about the visitor having an authentic-feeling experience than in exhibiting factually correct artifacts, performance rituals, and narratives.

The process of turning Lindsborg into a heritage site took more than thirty years, from the 1960s to the 1990s. These efforts engendered a number of discussions about what was authentically Swedish, and what public activities represented a faithful representation of local Swedish culture. Older residents of the town feared that the special Swedish culture was being lost, citing in particular the reduction in the number of residents who could speak Swedish. The efforts to be authentic were not backed up by rigorous academic study of Swedish culture. When there was a debate over authentic folk dancing in the 1970s, a group from Lindsborg traveled to Sweden and were surprised to learn that the various artifacts of Swedish presented in Lindsborg culture differed considerably from what they found in Sweden. When there were questions about which aspects of Swedish culture to adopt, they settled on what they imagined to be nineteenth-century Swedish peasant culture, ignoring the many changes that had occurred in Swedish culture since then, and also ignoring the regional variations one would find in Sweden. By the 2010s, many of the Swedish festivals held in Lindsborg included a large element of small-town American parade culture. This seemed to be just fine with the citizens of Lindsborg. In part, this was because there was not an ideal of Swedish culture and life against which portrayals were measured for correctness. Instead, there was an evolving, fluid notion of what constituted Swedishness. Once-and-for-all authenticity remained a continuously unfulfilled aspiration. It has often been ignored that, while this image of Swedishness was part of the community's self-identity and valuable to the local economy, it was not the defining characteristic of life in Lindsborg. The majority of people went about their everyday lives, working in the agricultural sector or at the local college, for example; and increasingly small percentages of the Lindsborg population actually had a direct blood line connection to Sweden.

Let us next turn to issues of authenticity and misinformation in Colonial Williamsburg. While the chief advocate of building Colonial Williamsburg (Reverend Goodwin) was a respected member of town, the plan for the heritage site was extremely disruptive to the citizens, for example, hundreds of homes were purchased and repurposed or destroyed, and many families had to be relocated. This effort to build a heritage site was possible, not only because of the deep pockets of the Rockefeller family, but also because the town was economically stagnating in the 1920s and desperate for jobs in the heart of the Great Depression of the 1930s. Buy-in to this heritage site was locally supported primarily for labor and economic reasons, and for some because Colonial Williamsburg brought urban renewal. The creation of the site had some unwelcome consequences, in particular the segregation of the Black community and the eventual flight of many Blacks from town.

Goodwin's plan had two main precepts, and these both had significant impact on issues of authenticity. The first precept was that Colonial Williamsburg was intended to be an homage to the patriotic acts of the founding fathers, to educate and inspire future people about the meaning of American patriotism. The impact here is that, at least well into the 1960s, the focus was on the wealthy White town leaders to the exclusion of other members of the community (women, free and enslaved Blacks, trades people, etc.). This clearly did not lead to an authentic representation of what life was like in eighteenth-century Williamsburg for most people.

Goodwin's second precept was to identify authenticity with historical exactitude. This was a risky strategy because a single incorrect fact would not only allow the visitor to say that the heritage site was inaccurate in that particular aspect, but also would psychologically cause the visitor to wonder whether there were additional factual errors in the Williamsburg recreation. There were many reasons that Williamsburg could not and even should not follow this second precept: there were thousands of details to get historically correct, ample missing documentation and too few original artifacts to be able to furnish the entire village correctly, some aspects of historical correctness would make for a poor visitor experience (e.g., muddy streets), and so on. But given that Colonial Williamsburg followed this precept of historical exactitude over the decades, it had to create what one scholar called *credibility armor*. This involved unprecedented levels of research on the buildings and furnishings of town, and rhetorical devices of dissembling and making excuses (pointing out to visitors that the staff had made historical mistakes, that it worked hard to correct them, that it could point to mistakes it had corrected, and that it promised to seek out and correct and future or undetected historical mistakes).

Although the Rockefellers bought in to Goodwin's precepts, they had a strong appreciation for the finer things in life, what we have called here an *elite aesthetic*; and this at times conflicted with total historical accuracy plan of Colonial Williamsburg. When the Rockefellers purchased a house on the historic site to live in part time, they furnished it not with artifacts that had been made in Colonial Williamsburg or were owned by people of Colonial Williamsburg. Instead, they furnished it with museum-quality artifacts from a time period that extended well beyond the eighteenth century and beyond the geographic region of Tidewater Virginia. Thus, the chief financial backer of Colonial Williamsburg was undermining the precept of historical exactitude. This issue was eventually resolved by a release valve strategy, creating two museums at the edge of Colonial Williamsburg to hold these finer things that did not meet Goodwin's precept of historical exactitude.

Lindsborg's debates over what constitutes authentic heritage were carried out by the ordinary citizens of their town. Williamsburg's debates were instead carried out largely by highly educated professionals, for example, historians, architects, and conservators both on the staff and on advisory boards. Trends in historical scholarship never touched what was done to the heritage site in Lindsborg, but it did have a profound effect on the direction of Colonial Williamsburg. The new social history that swept across America in the 1960s and 1970s led to a radical change in the mission of Colonial Williamsburg when the heritage site began hiring employees with this training. While the site would continue to tell the story of the founding fathers, as it had told it so well for more than forty years, it would now begin to also tell the stories of other members of the eighteenth-century Williamsburg community— women, slaves, tradespeople, the incarcerated, the mentally disadvantaged, and so on. And to some scholars, the stories of the wealthy White men should not receive privileged place among these other demographic groups who lived in eighteenth-century Williamsburg.

Williamsburg, in part because of its affiliation with the fundamental principles of the American Revolution, with major figures in American society such as the Rockefellers, and because of its position as the largest historic town reconstruction in the United States, has been the target of substantial criticism from outside scholars, especially with respect to its authenticity. We identified six types of criticisms from scholars: (1) compromises to the historic site because it was being used for contemporary purposes by both staff (who needed trash cans and electricity) and tourists (who needed mud-less streets and shade from the summer sun); (2) historical inadequacies (historical inaccuracies in recipes, among other examples); (3) focus on the wealthy, White male population with other groups only treated in regard to how they interacted with the wealthy Whites; (4) tensions between history as indisputable facts that are part of a master narrative in contrast to the belief that history is about interpretation, which is constructed by humans for many reasons (some conscious, some not) with various assumptions and agendas; (5) overdetermining the presentations, leaving nothing to the visitor's imagination; and (6) giving too much weight to entertainment rather than educational purposes—making the site, for some critics, like Disneyland, more a place of fantasy than truth.

Some scholars argue that authenticity is as much or more about experience (a subjective emergence into a heritage setting) than it is about the objective historical accuracy of artifacts and narratives. We have followed the work of two scholars who have explored the notion of experiential authenticity in Colonial Williamsburg. One used the lens of phenomenology to tease out five stages that lead the visitor to immersion in Williamsburg to the point they feel they have had an authentic experience, that they know what it was like to live in eighteenth-century Williamsburg. The other scholar has explored the important role of objects, not as items with a flawless historical provenance but instead as enablers of their experience. This scholar points out that, sometimes, reproductions can be more valuable to having an authentic experience than original objects because the originals may have secondary characteristics that distract one from gaining this immersive experience.

The final point of the discussion of authenticity in Colonial Williamsburg is that the notion of authenticity was commodified by the managers of Colonial Williamsburg for economic purposes. When a mid-priced maker of furniture created a line of Williamsburg reproduction furniture, this seriously undermined the heritage site's plans to create and sell its own high-end line of reproduction furniture. Colonial Williamsburg argued that its line of furniture was more authentic, despite the fact that it was made from machine-made parts and that the effort to create a furniture shop on the premises of Colonial Williamsburg largely failed (not able to make its own furniture but only assemble the machine-made pieces on site and then still requiring some electrified tools that were hidden in the back of the workshop, out of public view). This commodification strategy never worked well for Colonial

Williamsburg, whose products were too expensive, too demanding on the high-end department stores that served as their distribution system, and out of favor once American furniture tastes moved to a more modern style after the war. But it is an ironic story that Colonial Williamsburg tried to twist their story to claim that they were at an advantage because their furniture was more authentic.

What about authenticity in Gettysburg? The many people who visited or profited from Gettysburg expected the site to have a narrative that provided them with a moral lesson. Visitors began to visit the site only a few months after the battle was over, and they have been coming ever since. The site has always resonated not only with details of the battles, but also with larger issues about the Civil War and about race in American society. The stakes were higher in Gettysburg than in Lindsborg or Williamsburg because the experience was personal for many of the visitors, who had fought in or were friends or family of those who had fought in the war.

Historical accuracy was expected, but it was only a constraint on the moral lesson being offered, not the driving force behind it. Most visitors expected the park rangers to be knowledgeable (and they generally were)—and there was more trust in what they had to say than, for example, the costumed interpreters at Williamsburg. This trust in historical correctness was generally present even when, for example, a visitor from the South questioned the interpretations of the rangers, which some regarded as too pro-Union. So, to some degree, factual information and interpretation have been separated in the acceptance of what was presented at Gettysburg. Even more than the rangers answering questions on the battle sites, the museum was regarded as historically accurate and the artifacts displayed as authentic.

Even though many of the facts told about Gettysburg have remained constant over time, the messaging has evolved. For example, the stories about Robert E. Lee told over time become less flattering, even as messages of Reconciliation persisted.

Like Williamsburg, after the new social history reached Gettysburg in the 1970s, and constructivism, the belief that people construct and shape their perceived knowledge of a subject rather than passively accepting someone else's master narrative, was much on the minds of the staff and some of the visitors to Gettysburg. Constructivism reshapes the narrative, and the fact that there have been hundreds of books written about Gettysburg—each with its slightly different interpretation of events—shows this constructivism at work.

The National Park Service, when it took over Gettysburg in the 1930s, aspired to rigorous historical research, to being good empiricists as they developed and confirmed the interpretations they presented in their writings and their messages to the visitors, as they checked the provenance and descriptions of the artifacts they acquired, conserved, and displayed. This meant that the national park site was sometimes cautious of cooperating with other private museums that were also trading upon the Gettysburg story but perhaps with less care and research. The level of historical accuracy was much higher at Gettysburg than at Lindsborg, for example.

LESSONS FROM TOURISM AND INFORMATION SCHOLARSHIP

The material above presents some of the things we have learned about authenticity from the three case studies. Now let us turn to what we learned about authenticity from the theorizing by tourism scholars, which we discussed in the second half of chapter 1 (some key theories from tourism studies about authenticity) and most of chapter 2 (a survey of tourism scholarship for historical development of a conceptual understanding of authenticity).

Considering the material from chapter 1, one point concerns the two different approaches to authenticity: authenticity as an experience and authenticity as a product characteristic. The former is subjective, about the tourist's emotional response to a heritage environment; while the latter is objective, about whether the site correctly portrays the heritage events through "real" artifacts, factually correct narratives, and historically faithful environments.

Another major idea in this theory literature concerns the different ways in which a heritage site manifests its authenticity: the presentation of actual artifacts (object-related authenticity), the correctness of presentations (factual authenticity), whether the heritage sites accurately portrays the people and their role in the heritage narrative (personage authenticity), whether the reenactment occurs where the historic events actually happened (locational authenticity), and whether the environment in which the reenactment is made is faithful to the original environment, for example, without commercialization or urbanization not consonant with the original pastoral scene (contextual authenticity).

A third major idea from this theory literature concerns tourism imaginaries, the process by which an unassuming environment is transformed into a narrative account that effectively conveys to the tourist what happened at that heritage site that made it so important. The elements of this social construction of the tourism imaginary, the theorists claim, are: narrative; moral valuation of the past—that is, using history to teach moral lessons of relevance today; reinforcement through emplaced enactment, which allows the tourist to actively engage in the past activity; and emotional attachment between the story from the past and the visitor's present life.

Chapter 2 provided an overview of the research on authenticity and heritage tourism, and its chronological development, by examining one leading journal, the *Annals of Tourism Research*, over its fifty-year history. We identified three overarching themes through that survey. One concerned understanding—the tension between factual understanding of a site and the desire to promote a more positive image, for example, for economic gain or better self-image. A second theme concerned presentation, the issues that arose as a heritage community attempted to offer an educational experience to visitors in an authentic manner. The third theme concerned the disruptive force of the Internet, for example, as tourists and others discussed their heritage experiences online and whether they were authentic.

The word 'authentic' was not used in the early tourism literature. Nevertheless, the concept arose regularly, using such terms as "phony folk culture," especially in studies of business motivations to exploit cultural heritage and the harmful effect they may have had on the residents whose culture was being exploited. A more recent argument made by these tourism scholars was that authenticity must be created for a heritage site as a means to distance tourists from their everyday lives. As one scholar said, authenticity "is the respectable child of old-fashioned exoticism."[1,2] For example, anthropologist John P. Taylor pointed to the multiple meanings of authenticity, seeing the concept as the interaction between the tourist and the heritage object, between the here and now. He was more interested in the related notion of sincerity, which would lead to a shift in "moral perspectives" largely away from whatever locates tourism's value in the reproduction of objects and experiences, toward a form of tourism that communicates values deemed important to the providers of these experiences.

Numerous studies by tourism scholars identified examples of authenticity at heritage sites, and there has been considerable discussion of "staged authenticity"—that is, how to conduct reenactments at heritage sites that were deemed authentic. Much has been made in these scholarly discussions about what really happened in these past events being presented and the ways in which the providers of the tourism experience provided idealized images of traditions that were more in keeping with how residents of the area saw themselves or their histories, or which were more comfortable to the tourists who did not want to confront unpleasant realities, for example, about the treatment of Blacks or Native Americans. A feeling of authenticity is achieved, these scholars argued, in these cases by providing certain forms of experience that tourists expect, for example, concerning food or dance, observing crafts being created, and having mementos of their experience they can take home with them. In these situations, the facts themselves or the evaluations of objective experts (historians, anthropologists) are not the basis of authenticity; instead, authenticity rests in the judgments of the tourists, the providers of the tourist experience, and the media. Moreover, the sense of authenticity is dependent on the characteristics of the tourist population—what might be authentic for an older, wealthier, better educated group of tourists might not be seen as authentic by inner city school children or college students on Spring Break. Since 2016, tourism scholars have been trying to connect their work to the burgeoning research in many academic disciplines concerning fake facts and fake news.

Turning now to the overarching theme of presentation, we have seen numerous studies in the tourism studies literature about two issues: whether the industry's activities appeal to tourists, especially ones who aspire to historical, educational heritage experiences; and how best to conceptualize the notion of authenticity. Much of this scholarship relates to the physical nature of authenticity—its connection to space, place, and culture.

By the turn of the century, the scholarly literature on heritage tourism was often concerned with the flow of information and how it was presented. New concepts were introduced: "object-related authenticity" focusing on artifacts and buildings and their impact on tourist experiences, "constructed experience" which focused on the form of authenticity that is projected on to what a tourist sees or hears (i.e., socially constructed and not inherent in the objects they observe), and "activity-related authenticity" concerning the experiences of tourists as they interact with the heritage site. Scholars conducted both empirical and theoretical analyses that raised questions about the surface beliefs of tourists and locals regarding what they were thinking and wanting. The field has adopted a multiplicity of perspectives, both practical and theoretical, and over time a substantial body of literature built up, to connect their new studies to. In the eyes of some tourism scholars, the definition of authenticity "remains conceptually contested and has taken few steps towards becoming an 'anchor' for a tourism paradigm."[3] Some recent scholarship, importantly, has moved away from the authenticity of objects to the process by which objects or sites are authenticated. An important distinction has emerged in the literature between rational and speculative ways of knowing. "Cool authentication" is about emotionally detached, rationally established processes, with experts as the final arbiters, to identify the authenticity of objects and places. "Hot authentication" is about personal, emotionally based recognition of objects as authentic. Authentication arises from performative, often affective acts related to tourists' experiences and beliefs, often involving the performance of rituals.[4] This new focus enables scholars to turn from a description or analysis of the tourists' experiences to a more sociological explanation of the process by which a tourist accomplishes an experience they regard as authentic.

The third overarching theme concerns the disruptive impact of the Internet on tourism. The Internet is an important tool for providers to market tourism sites, to present their vision and shape potential visitor's expectations of what will happen if they visit the heritage site. However, in this era of the interactive Internet and social media, visitors and professional travel writers can themselves participate in conversations about the heritage site: how do they portray the site? is it an enjoyable and entertaining experience? In which ways is it authentic or inauthentic? Some scholars have been studying the affordances of different websites and social networking sites, and in what ways these differences attract particular kinds of audiences and shape the kind of discussions that occur there. Inasmuch as the Internet knows no geographical boundaries, there is now an increasing participation of scholars from around the world, not just from North America and Western Europe, and this introduces new examples and new perspectives that are refreshing the body of scholarship. This interest in the medium of the Internet has also attracted a new set of scholars from media studies and communication studies to join in the conversation.

CHAPTER 6

Let us now turn to questions about the interactions between tourism scholars and information scholars. Consider first the general connections between these two fields. While tourism is an information-rich activity, tourism studies have generally not focused explicitly on information issues other than some studies of tourism information management systems. Nevertheless, there are some significant similarities between the two fields. Cultural tourism is often an exercise in education, imparting information and knowledge to visitors. Museums and artefacts are studied by both fields. The everyday engagement of humans with information is at the heart of information behavior, a central field in information studies. Unlike many of the pure social science and humanities disciplines, but like some of the applied disciplines, both information studies and tourism studies involve not only academic scholars but also practitioners (librarians, tourism managers). In both fields, practitioners set agendas, ground discussions in practical everyday activities, and interact with their more theoretical colleagues.

What about the connections, more specifically, between information scholars' study of misinformation and tourism scholars' study of (in) authenticity? The study of misinformation by information scholars has, so far, been structured around well-established topical areas (e.g., information behavior, libraries) or well-established research methods (e.g., computational methods, such as natural language processing and machine learning). In other words, misinformation is not so much a new domain of scholarship for information scholars – with its own concepts, frameworks, and methods—as it is an application of existing ways of thinking within information studies applied to a hot contemporary topic. Perhaps tourism studies can stimulate new ways for information scholars to approach misinformation. Another reason for hope here is that much of the scholarship in information studies draws upon psychology and sociology, whereas tourism studies has drawn extensively on other disciplines such as anthropology and geography, so perhaps tourism studies can help information studies to broaden its foundations.

While there is already some study of the economics of information, tourism provides an excellent example of where a practical information environment is mediated by economic considerations, and where these economic concerns often cause tensions over authenticity of artifacts and experience. Place is an important element of tourism studies on authenticity, but currently it comes up only occasionally in information studies, for example, in the design of library spaces. Many of the heritage sites studied by information scholars are educational institutions; in this education mission, they are similar to the libraries, museums, and archival collections studied by information scholars. These educational institutions face similar issues in both fields of study: intended audiences, roles in their local communities, augmentations of the formal education system for children, tensions between perceived traditional narratives and alternative narratives (sometimes involving underrepresented populations), tensions between the worship of the artifact and the focus on its interpretation, and questions over real versus staged authenticity. In recent years, both tourism studies and information studies have considered activities that take place not in physical spaces (libraries, heritage sites) but instead online, involving both suppliers (tourism site managers, local economic development officers, travel writers, booksellers, authors) and consumers (tourists, locals, readers).

The study of the social construction of knowledge began in information studies in the 1950s, but it is still not a major line of inquiry. In recent years, tourism scholars have increasingly focused on the process of authentication instead of evaluation of whether facts or artifacts are authentic. One can imagine that the information scholars can learn from the tourism scholars not about whether a fact is fake, or how it enhances a power relationship, but instead focuses on the process by which particular populations, for example, QAnon followers, accept some things as facts but not others.

APPLYING THESE LESSONS

In one sense, the goal of this study has been to extend upon a set of books and articles we have produced on misinformation, in various forms, from various perspectives. In fact, we have studied or pointed to misinformation as it has existed in more than two hundred years of American history, as it has been scrutinized by an unlikely group of showmen and magicians, as it has persisted in myths about the old American West and urban legends about the 9/11 terrorist attacks, and how it compares to art and literary forgeries. One can certainly extend the study of misinformation by examining other domains where misinformation occurs regularly but which are far removed from the fake facts that have appeared in newspapers, social networking sites, and political speeches that have been so exhaustively covered by many types of scholars in the past seven years. With an eye sensitized to identify misinformation, opportunities to study it exist in many areas. Obvious to your authors are real estate industry redlining practices, military beliefs that continue to include studying some lessons at military academies drawn from Napoleon that have not been effectively useful since the dawn of military mechanization during the First and Second World Wars, and the ongoing but sometimes questionable scientific evidence presented by the pharmaceutical industry and the academic researchers it funds (echoing the findings about the tobacco and petroleum industries in our book *Fake News Nation* [2019]). In each of these instances, and many others, scholars embedded in relevant disciplines have lessons to teach information scholars through both their scholarship and methodologies.

Another reason for this study is to suggest to information scholars that there is a lot to learn from other kinds of disciplinary and interdisciplinary studies. What can information scholars learn from the tourism scholars? While there are, no doubt, many specific approaches that information scholars can gain from reading individual articles about tourism, we point to five main lessons we can draw from the tourism literature that we have surveyed that may assist the information scholar in learning about misinformation.

- One lesson is the change in focus of the tourism scholars from the characteristic of being authentic to the process of authentification. One can imagine that the information scholar may gain deeper insight by not merely focusing on whether a fact is true or false but instead look at the process of both creation and evaluation of the truth or "truthiness" of an assertion. To use the hot-cool distinction of the tourism scholars, the information studies scholars have overwhelmingly studied cool misinformation and largely ignored hot misinformation.
- A second lesson is something we have discussed in this book as the fluidity of information over time. Changing economic and social realities affected the information regarded as true at a given time; and when residents of Lindsborg described new or more subtle pieces of information, this can be regarded as less an attack on supposedly false or misinformed knowledge and practices of the past, and more readily as part of a mindset consistent with their current realities. The concept of fluidity is more than another way of describing that information and points-of-view evolve. Rather, the

idea suggests that there is a constant transformation of information and perspectives occurring that seem subtle, imperceptible, so tiny that one might find it difficult to identify when happening. Facts flow through the psyche of a town in the way water flows in a river, moving, changing as it does so, but impossible to differentiate from what it was a few minutes earlier upstream. Information scholars may have to think through how to deal with that reality because it probably makes sense to assume that, at the individual level within a community, views are changing microscopically in real time. This is one instance of the social construction of knowledge, which has received relatively little attention from information scholars.

- A third lesson for the information scholars is the value of ethnography to provide detailed case studies We have seen that these ethnographic studies, such as those concerning Lindsborg that we have reported on, provide us with ample information about the contextual factors such as space, place, and culture to enable us to understand why the re-creation of life in the Mother Country has developed as it has, and why residents and tourists accept or denounce various aspects of it as authentic. One can imagine that the information scholar will have a better understanding of misinformation as it appears in political environments if we understand not only the detailed motivations of the political operative but also the space, place, and culture of the audience.

- Fourth, the tourism scholarship shows us the importance of examining case studies that are taken from places other than North America, Western Europe, and Eastern Asia; as well as the worth of gaining insights and perspectives from a worldwide community of scholarly voices. These case studies and the authors who are writing them provide the traditional information scholar with a better realization of the importance of place, space, and culture in the topics they are studying.

- A final lesson is that most of the disciplinary work drawn upon in information studies is based in sociology or psychology. The tourism scholars have drawn on psychology and sociology, but also on other social science and humanities disciplines, including economics, geography, anthropology, and folklore studies. There may be opportunities for information scholars to learn from the use of disciplinary ways of thinking adopted by the interdisciplinary tourism scholars.

NOTES

1. Salman Rushdie, *Imaginary Homelands: Essays and Criticism, 1981–1991* (London: Granta, 1991), 67.

2. Rushdie, *Imaginary Homelands*, 67.

3. Moore et al., "Authenticity in Tourism and Experience. Practically Indispensable and Theoretically Mischievous?" 1.

4. Erik Cohen and Scott A. Cohen, "Authentication: Hot and Cool," *Annals of Tourism Research* 39, no. 3 (2012): 1295–314.

INDEX

Page references for figures are italicized.

gardens, of Williamsburg, 77, 81, 88
Gardner, Alexander, 7
GBMA. *See* Gettysburg Battlefield
  Memorial Association
genealogical research, Swedish, 56,
  62
George Floyd, 108
Gettysburg, 10, 11-12, 114, 144n4,
  156-69; administration as, 136;
  African Americans visiting,
  131-32; authenticity and,
  141-44, 161; judges of events
  at, 111-13; landscaping at,
  112, 115, 145n11; Lost Cause,
  126-29; museums at, 136,
  137-38; mythology around, 113;
  narrative of, 136; NPS and, 135,
  154-55, 162; preservation and,
  133-40; race and, 121; slavery
  and, 127-28; soldiers at, 110-11;
  tourists at, 110, 142; violence
  and trauma and, 129-31; visitors
  at, *140*, 141. *See also* battle, at
  Gettysburg
Gettysburg Address, 111, *119-20*
Gettysburg Battlefield Memorial
  Association (GBMA), 121
Gettysburg-battle-specific objects,
  110
Gettysburg Museum, 137-38
ghost stories, 143
gift shops, 57, 63
globalization, economic, 21-22
Gone with the Wind (film), 128
Goodwin, W. A. R., 72, 75-79, 86, 95,
  98n9, 157-59
Governor's Palace, 79, *80*
Grand Army of the Republic (GAR),
  125
Great Depression, 74, 79, 82
Greenwood, D. J., 21
groups, authentic, 6

"hallowed ground," 123
Hampton, Ronald, 94
Handler, Richard, 78, 83
handshaking event, 125
Harris, Dave, 12n6
health misinformation, 34
Heidegger, Martin, 12n6
heritage, viii, ix; authenticity of, 58;
  debates on, 159; ethnic, 62
heritage buildings, 23
heritage experience, for tourists,
  25-27
heritage festivals, 59
heritage sites, viii, 162-63;
  attendance of, 154; building, 157-
  58; large private, 69-70; small, 47;
  sustained history of, 154; travel to,
  52; types of, 5. *See also specific sites*
Heritage Square, in Lindsborg, 56, 63
heritage studies, 27
heritage tourism, viii, 2, 13n11
heritage tourism scholars, 9-12
heroes, dead, 121-25
hero worship, 85
"High Water Mark" myth, 118,
  147n29
historians, 85, 135-36
historical accuracy, 77, 83, 95, 161
historical clothing, 76, *80*
historical correctness, 158
historical exactitude, authenticity
  and, 75-78
historical inaccuracy, 76
historical inadequacies, 84
historical myth, 3, 14n14
historical scholarship, 159
Historic Area, 90
history: Black, 88, 95; cultural,
  156; imagination and, 85-86; as
  interpretation, 85; new social,
  86-88, 95; reimagination of, 7
holidays, 52

new social history, 86–88, 95

9/11 terrorist attacks, 167–68

nostalgia, desire for, 23

NPS. *See* National Park Service

object-related authenticity, 10, 26, 37, 164

objects, 6, 91; Gettysburg-battle-specific, 110; military, 135

Old Mill Museum, 56

"Old World" look, 59

olfactory, 90

O'Toole, Dennis, 88

parades, local, 58

park rangers, 121

parks, national, 134

patriotism, 86, 95, 130

peasant lifestyle, idealized, 58

peer-reviewed scholarly journals, 19

personage authenticity, 115

personas, authentic, 6

perspective, postcolonial, 32

Peterson, Richard A., 7

phony folk-culture, 21, 163

photographs, staged, 7–8

Pickett's Charge, 117, 125, 138

plantations, 131–32

plasticity, of information, 156

Plimouth Plantation, 92

political fact-checking, vii

political misinformation, 34

population, of Williamsburg, 71

postcolonial perspective, 32

post-disciplinary thought, 38n11

postmodernism, 26

Poststructuralism, 22

poverty, 81

presentation, 20

preservations, and authenticity, 133–40

presidential election, 2016, vii, 34

product feature, 114; authenticity as, 10, 162

professional experts, 7, 8

pseudo-events, 8

psychological effects, of combat, 130

psychology, 169

QAnon, 37, 167

race, 141, 154; authenticity and, 133; discourse on, 116; Gettysburg and, 121; slavery and, 131–33; Williamsburg and, 86–88

racial ideology, 127

racial inequality, 108

racism, 108; Civil War and, 129–30, 131; Jim Crow, 126

Raleigh Tavern, 93

Recipes from America's Restored Villages (cookbook), 84

reconciliation, 125–26, 130, 132, 135; narrative of, 139–40

Reconstruction, 132

reenactments, 136; of battle, 116

reimagination, of history, 7

religion, 75

religious language, 122

renovations, at Williamsburg, 79, 81

reproduction furniture, 81, 92, 105n71, 160–61

research methods, 28

residents, displaced, 73

revenue generation, 49

rights, of African American, 127–28

Rockefeller, Abby, 78

Rockefeller, John D. Jr., 71, 78–83, 86, 98n9, 103n56, 158

Roosevelt, Franklin, 79

Salet, Xavier, 40n43

Schmitz, Hermann, 89

scholars: on authenticity, 27–28; authenticity research, 34–37;

ABOUT THE AUTHORS

William Aspray is senior research fellow at the Charles Babbage Institute, a research institute for the study of computing, information, and culture at the University of Minnesota. He has previously taught in the information schools at Colorado (Boulder), Texas (Austin), and Indiana (Bloomington)—and also at Harvard and Williams. He has also served in senior management positions at the IEEE History Center, the Babbage Institute, and the Computing Research Association. He has served as the editor in chief of the journal *Information & Culture*. His most relevant books, both of them written together with James Cortada, are *Fake News Nation* (Rowman & Littlefield, 2019) and *From Urban Legends to Political Fact-Checking* (2019).

James W. Cortada is a senior research fellow at the Charles Babbage Institute, University of Minnesota, and the coauthor with William Aspray of *Fake News Nation*. He is the author of *Building Blocks of Society: History, Information Ecosystems, and Infrastructures* (Rowman & Littlefield, 2020), as well as numerous other books on computers, information, and technology.